Language Helper German

Helping You Speak *More* German

Therese Slevin Pirz

and

Mark Hobson

Chou Chou Press
4 Whimbrel Court Bluffton SC 29909
www.Bilingualkids.com

Cataloging data: Pirz, Therese Slevin
           Language helper – German: Helping you speak
           more German.
           Chou Chou Press, 2008
           209 p. illus.
           Description: A collection of basic German conversational
           phrases and their translation arranged in alphabetical order.

           1. ESL – English as a second language 2. German language
           3. German phrases 4.German conversation and phrase
           book 5. Homeschooling
           I. Title. II. Title: Helping you speak more German.
           III. Series: Language helper
           II. Author. Mark Hobson   430

Printed in the United States of America, 2008

First Edition.

ISBN   978-0-9789152-0-9

Order direct from the publisher:

                 Chou Chou Press
                 4 Whimbrel Court
                 Bluffton SC 29909
                 www.Bilingualkids.com

Language Helper
German

Thy will be done on earth
As it is in heaven.
Dein Wille geschehe
Wie im Himmel auch auf Erden.

Table of Contents

Acknowledgement

I wish to thank Mark Hobson for his enthusiasm, thoroughness and professionalism in the production of this text. Mark has been an invaluable translator.

I am likewise grateful to Friedhelm and Irmgard Schlaf for their contributions to this text. I appreciate their time, efforts and expertise.

I am sure you will be pleased with the results.

A quick acknowledgement, too, to all those – parents, teachers, and librarians – who see the need for learning foreign languages in this world of ours, and are doing something about it. Keep up the good work!

Preface

<u>Language Helper – German</u> is the next book for those who are already familiar with <u>Kids Stuff German</u>. Like <u>Kids Stuff German</u>, this book is designed as a basis for forming additional constructions anticipated by the user. This book is arranged in alphabetical order rather than by topic. Hopefully, this dictionary format will enable the user to quickly pinpoint the exact sentence needed.

We know many people have enjoyed <u>Kids Stuff German</u> and found it very useful. We trust that the same reaction will greet <u>Language Helper – German</u>.

Notes

Words in *italics* indicate an idiomatic and not a literal meaning of the word. These words are selected for the convenience of the user, and are not to be construed as an exact translation of the German meaning.

The definite article (der, die, das) indicates the gender of the noun.

Check the oil, the water, the battery!
Schau dem Ol,dem Wasser, der Batterie nach!
Shaou daim erhl, daim VAHS-sehr, dehr bah-tehr-REE nakh!

Step on it!
Gib Gas!
Ghip gas!

Fill 'er up!
Auftanken!
AOUF-tahn-k'n!

A

I'm just **about** to fix breakfast.   about – ger<u>a</u>de
Ich w<u>o</u>llte ger<u>a</u>de das Fr<u>ü</u>hstück m<u>a</u>chen.

It's the other way **about** (around).   *– about –*
Es ist ger<u>a</u>de <u>u</u>mgekehrt.   <u>u</u>mgekehrt – just the opposite

I'm not **about** to let you watch   *– about*
that TV program!   w<u>o</u>llen – want
Ich will nicht, daß du dir ger<u>a</u>de d<u>ie</u>se F<u>e</u>rnsehsendung <u>a</u>nsiehst.

I've had **about** enough of this.   *– about*
Jetzt r<u>ei</u>cht es mir <u>a</u>ber allm<u>ä</u>hlich.   allm<u>ä</u>hlich – gradual(ly)

AAA AA AAA AA AAA AA AAA AA AAA AA AAA AA AAA

There are toys lying all **about** the room. — *about*
Die Spielsachen liegen überall im   herumliegen – to lie around
Zimmer herum.

While you're **about** it...   — *about*
Wenn du schon dabei bist...   dabei – with it

That's **about** it.   — *about*
Das ist so ziemlich alles.   alles – everything

What **about** me?   — *about*
Und ich? Und was ist mit mir?   mit mir – with me

Do you think you're **above** all that?   — *above*
Du meinst, du stehst darüber?   darüber – above it

You cannot be **absent** from school.   absent – abwesend
Du darfst in der Schule nicht abwesend sein.

Absolutely! (Not)   absolutely – genau
Genau! (Nicht)

You've been **absorbed**   to be absorbed in – sich vertiefen in
in that book for hours!
Du bist seit Stunden in das Buch vertieft.

Don't be **absurd**!   absurd – albern
Sei nicht albern!

I want to make it **abundantly** clear.   — *abundantly*
Ich will es überdeutlich zu   überdeutlich – overly clear
verstehen geben.

You must **accept** responsibility.   to accept – übernehmen
Du mußt manchmal die Verantwortung übernehmen.

10

AAA AA AAA AA AAA AA AAA AA AAA AA AAA AA AAA

That behavior is not **acceptable**.
Das Benehmen ist nicht zulässig.

acceptable – zulässig

This is no **accident**.
Das ist kein Zufall.

accident – der Zufall

That didn't **accomplish** anything.
Damit war nichts erreicht.

– *accomplish*
erreichen – to reach

I'll take that into **account**.
Ich werde das in Betracht ziehen.

– *account*
der Betracht – consideration

On no **account** do you leave
your sister alone.
Auf keinen Fall sollst du deine Schwester allein lassen.

– *account*
der Fall – case

I can't **account for** it.
Ich kann das nicht erklären.

– *account for*
erklären – to explain

Are you **accusing** me of lying?
Willst du vielleicht sagen, daß ich lüge?

– *accuse*
sagen – to say

I **ache** all over!
Mir tut alles weh!

to ache – wehtun

Asparagus, it's an **acquired** taste.
Der Spargel, das ist eine
Geschmackssache.

– *acquired*
die Geschmackssache –
matter of taste

Don't run **across** the road!
Lauf nicht über die Straße!

across – über

It's all an **act**!
Das ist alles nur Schau!

act – die Schau

AAA AA AAA AA AAA AA AAA AA AAA AA AAA AA AAA

You're **acting**/ silly/ stupid/.
Du stellst dich dumm.

to act – sich stellen

Act your age!
Sei nicht kindisch!

– *to act*
kindisch – childish

Now is the time for **action**!
Die Zeit zum Handeln ist jetzt gekommen!

action – handeln

What were his **actual** words?
Was hat er genau gesagt?

actual(ly) – genau

Don't tell me you're **actually** studying!
Sag mir bloß nicht, daß du jetzt wirklich lernst!

actually – wirklich

Add the numbers.
Rechne die Zahlen zusammen!

to add – zusammenrechnen

It's beginning to **add up.**
Jetzt wird so manches klar.

– *to add up*
klar – clear

Without further **ado.**
Ohne Weiteres.

– *ado*
Weiteres – further ado

I must **admit** that you were right.
Ich gebe zu, du hattest recht.

to admit – zugeben

You're very **advanced** for your age.
Du bist für dein Alter sehr fortgeschritten.

advanced –
fortgeschritten

She's taking **advantage** of you!
Sie nutzt dich aus!

advantage – ausnutzen

Let me give you a piece of **advice**!
Darf ich dir einen Rat geben!

advice – der Rat

12

AAA AA AAA AA AAA AA AAA AA AAA AA AAA AA AAA

I'd **advise** you to study hard.　　　　　　to advise – r<u>a</u>ten
Ich w<u>ü</u>rde dir r<u>a</u>ten, fl<u>ei</u>ßig zu l<u>e</u>rnen.

And I use the word **advisedly**!　　　　　advisedly – <u>a</u>bsichtlic
Ich verw<u>e</u>nde <u>a</u>bsichtlich d<u>ie</u>ses Wort!

I can't **afford** to buy a new bicycle.　　　to afford – sich l<u>ei</u>sten
Ich kann mir ein n<u>eu</u>es F<u>a</u>hrrad nicht l<u>ei</u>sten.

I'm **afraid**/ so/ not.　　　　　　　　　– *afraid*
L<u>ei</u>der ist es so./ L<u>ei</u>der nicht/.　　l<u>ei</u>der – unfortunately

That was what I was **afraid of**.　　　　afraid of – bef<u>ü</u>rchtet
Das h<u>a</u>be ich bef<u>ü</u>rchtet.

Don't be **afraid** of making a mistake.　– *afraid of*
Hab k<u>ei</u>ne <u>A</u>ngst, <u>ei</u>nen F<u>e</u>hler zu m<u>a</u>chen!　<u>A</u>ngst h<u>a</u>ben –
　　　　　　　　　　　　　　　　　　　　　to have fear

After what has happened!　　　　　　– *after*
Nach <u>a</u>llem, was gesch<u>e</u>hen ist!　nach <u>a</u>llem – after everything

What are you **after**?　　　　　　　　– *after*
Was willst du?　　　　　　　　　　　　w<u>o</u>llen – want

Again and again. Not **again**!　　　　again – w<u>ie</u>der
<u>I</u>mmer w<u>ie</u>der. Schon w<u>ie</u>der!

Don't do that **again**!　　　　　　　　again – w<u>ie</u>der
Tu das nicht w<u>ie</u>der!

Spinach doesn't **agree** with me.　　　to agree – bek<u>o</u>mmen
Spin<u>a</u>t bek<u>o</u>mmt mir nicht.

13

AAA AA AAA AA AAA AA AAA AA AAA AA AAA AA AAA

I **agree** that I was wrong.　　　　　　　　– *agree*
Ich gebe zu, daß ich mich geirrt habe.　　zugeben – to admit

I quite **agree**!　　　　　　　　　　　– *agree*
Ganz meine Meinung!　　　　　　　　die Meinung – opinion

Agreed?　　　　　　　　　　　　agreed – einverstanden
Einverstanden?

I'll go on **ahead**.　　　　　　　　ahead – voraus
Ich werde vorausgehen.

Walk **ahead** of me.　　　　　　　ahead – voraus
Geh mir voraus.

Air out your room!　　　　　　　to air – lüften
Lüfte dein Zimmer!

You slept through the **alarm clock**.　alarm clock – der Wecker
Du hast den Wecker nicht gehört.

Don't be **alarmed**.　　　　　　　alarmed – erschrocken
Sei nicht erschrocken.

Be **alert**!　　　　　　　　　　　to alert – aufmerksam
Sei aufmerksam!

I want **all** of it.　　　　　　　　all – alles
Ich will alles.

That's **all** very well.　　　　　　all – alles
Das ist alles ganz schön und gut.

All right, all right, I'm coming!　all right – schon gut
Schon gut! Schon gut! Ich komme ja!

14

AAA AA AAA AA AAA AA AAA AA AAA AA AAA AA AAA

Is it **all right** for me to play outside?
Darf ich draußen spielen?

   – all right
dürfen – to be allowed

Are you feeling **all right**?
Fühlst du dich wohl?

   – all right
wohl – well

All the more so.
Um so mehr.

   – all the more
mehr – more

I won't **allow** you to do that.
Ich erlaube nicht, daß du das machst.

to allow – erlauben

You're not **allowed** to do that
Du darfst das nicht tun.

   – allow
dürfen – to be allowed

I did it all **alone**.
Ich habe es ganz allein getan.

alone – allein

You're thinking **aloud**.
Du redest vor dich hin.

   – aloud
reden – to talk

Absolutely **amazing**!
Wirklich erstaunlich!

amazing – erstaunlich

You certainly are **ambitious**!
Du bist sehr ehrgeizig!

ambitious – ehrgeizig

It **amounts** to the same thing.
Das kommt aufs gleiche hinaus.

   – to amount to
hinauskommen – to come to

You can **amuse** yourself for a while.
Du kannst dich eine Zeitlang selbst
unterhalten.

   – to amuse
sich unterhalten –
to amuse oneself

I am not **amused**!
Ich finde keinen Spaß daran!

   – to be amused
der Spaß – fun

AAA AA AAA AA AAA AA AAA AA AAA AA AAA AA AAA

You're an **angel**.
Du bist ein Engel.

angel – der Engel

You're/ **annoying** me/ making me angry/!
Du ärgerst mich!

to annoy – ärgern

Don't be so **annoying**!
Sei nicht so ärgerlich!

annoying – ärgerlich

Let's do it **another** way.
Machen wir es auf andere Art und Weise!

another – ander(e)

Without **another** word!
Ohne ein weiteres Wort!

– *another*
weiter – other, further

Don't **answer** me **back**!
Keine Widerrede!

– *to answer back*
die Widerrede – contradiction

Are you **anxious** about anything?
Bist du um etwas besorgt?

anxious – besorgt

I can do it without **any** help.
Ich kann es ohne jede Hilfe machen.

any – jed(e)

You're not just **anybody**.
Du bist nicht einfach irgend jemand.

anybody – irgend jemand

I don't want it done **anyhow** (carelessly).
Ich will nicht, daß man es schlampig macht.

– *anyhow*
schlampig – carelessly

Don't tell **anyone**!
Sag das keinem!

– *anyone*
keiner – no one

Did you have **anything** to do with it?
Hast du damit etwas zu tun gehabt?

anything – etwas

16

AAA AA AAA AA AAA AA AAA AA AAA AA AAA AA AAA

Is there **anything** the matter?
Ist etwas los?

anything – etwas

Anything could happen.
Irgend etwas könnte geschehen.

anything – irgend etwas

Have you seen my keys **anywhere**?
Hast du meine Schlüssel irgendwo gesehen?

anywhere – irgendwo

You're not getting **anywhere**.
Du kommst einfach nicht weiter.

– *anywhere*
weiterkommen – come forward

I owe you an **apology**.
Ich bin dir eine Entschuldigung schuldig.

apology – die
Entschuldigung

You owe me **apology**.
Du bist mir eine Entschuldigung schuldig.

apology – die
Entschuldigung

So it would **appear**.
So scheint es.

to appear – scheinen

You are the **apple of my eye**.
Du bist mein Liebling.

– *apple of one's eye*
der Liebling – darling

Apply yourself (to your work).
Streng dich (bei der Arbeit) an!

to apply – sich anstrengen

I **appreciate** your help.
Ich weiß deine Hilfe zu schätzen.

to appreciate – zu schätzen
wissen

I don't **approve** of your attitude.
Ich finde deine Einstellung nicht richtig.

– *to approve*
richtig finden –
to find correct

AAA AA AAA AA AAA AA AAA AA AAA AA AAA AA AAA

Don't **argue** with me!   – *argue*
Keine Widerrede!   die Widerrede – contradiction

Put your arm **around** me!   – *around*
Umarme mich!   umarmen – to hug

Did you look all **around**?   – *around*
Hast du nach allen Seiten herumgesehen?   herumsehen –
                                   to look around

That's **arranged** then!   arranged – abgemacht
Das ist dann abgemacht!

You're very **artistic**.   artistic – künstlerisch
Du bist künstlerisch veranlagt.

Leave it **as** it is.   – *as*
Laß es so.   lassen – to let be

Is it **as** difficult **as** that?   – *as*
Ist das denn so schwierig?   so – so

Do **as** much **as** you can!   – *as*
Tu soviel du kannst!   so – so

Do **as** you like.   – *as*
Mach, was du willst.   was – what(ever)

Ask away!   to ask – fragen
Frag los!

Don't **ask** me!   to ask – fragen
Frag mich nicht!

If it isn't **asking** too much…   to ask – verlangen
Wenn das nicht zuviel verlangt ist…

That's **asking** for trouble.   – *ask*
Das kann ja nicht g<u>u</u>tgehen.   g<u>u</u>tgehen – to go nicely

It's yours for the **asking**.   – *ask*
Du kannst es h<u>a</u>ben.   h<u>a</u>ben – to have

You have to **assert** yourself!   to assert oneself –
Du mußt dich d<u>u</u>rchsetzen!   sich d<u>u</u>rchsetzen

You're/ good/ bad/ **at** soccer.   at – im
Du bist/ gut/ schlecht/ im F<u>u</u>ßball.

At your age...   at – in
In d<u>ei</u>nem <u>A</u>lter...

You're a natural **athlete**.   athlete – der Sp<u>o</u>rtler
Du bist der geb<u>o</u>rene Sp<u>o</u>rtler.

Pay **attention**.   – *attention*
Paß auf!   <u>au</u>fpassen – to pay attention

You're not paying **attention**.   – *attention*
Du paßt nicht auf.   <u>au</u>fpassen – to pay attention

I don't like your **attitude**.   attitude – die <u>Ei</u>nstellung
D<u>ei</u>ne <u>Ei</u>nstellung gef<u>ä</u>llt mir nicht.

Why are you **avoiding** me?   to avoid – m<u>ei</u>den
Warum m<u>ei</u>dest du mich?

Stay **away** from/ him/ her/!   – *away*
Bleib von/ ihm/ ihr/ weg!   w<u>e</u>gbleiben – to stay away

Here I am!
Hier bin ich!
Heer bihn ihsh!

Are you surprised!
Bist du überrascht?
Bihst doo ih-behr-ASHT?

Look out! (s)
Paß auf!
Pahs owf

Look out! (pl)
Paßt auf!
Pahst owf

B

That's **baby** talk.
Das ist Babysprache.

baby – das Baby

Don't be such a **baby**!
Stell dich nicht so kindisch an!

– *baby*
anstellen – to act

Will you **babysit** for the little ones?
Willst du für die Kleinen babysitten?

to babysit – babysitten

Sit in the **back** of the car.
Setz dich hinten im Auto hin!

back – hinten

BB BBB BB BBB BB BBB BB BBB BB BBB BB BBB BB BBB

Backward and forward/ **back** and forth.   *back(ward)*
Hin und her.   *hin – away*

Stop walking **backwards**!   backwards – rückwärts
Hör auf, rückwarts zu gehen!

Your sweater is on **backwards**.   backwards – verkehrt
Dein Pullover ist verkehrt!

It would not be a **bad** thing!   bad – schlecht
Das wäre nicht schlecht!

I feel **bad**.   bad – schlecht
Mir geht es schlecht.

Things are going from **bad** to worse.   bad – schlimm
Es wird immer schlimmer.

It's not as **bad** as all that.   bad – schlimm
So schlimm ist es nun auch wieder nicht.

Don't feel **bad** about it.   *– bad*
Mach dir keine Gedanken darüber!   der Gedanke – thought

You didn't do so **badly**. (contest)   badly – schlecht
Du hast nicht so schlecht abgeschnitten.

You **baffle** me! (amaze)   *– to baffle*
Du bist mir ein Rätsel!   das Rätsel – puzzle

It's in the **bag**!   *– bag*
Das ist so gut wie sicher.   sicher – to be certain

Your pants look **baggy**.   baggy – ausgebeult
Deine Hose ist ausgebeult.

22

BB BBB BB BBB BB BBB BB BBB BB BBB BB BBB BB BBB

Don't lose your **balance**!
Verlier nicht das Gleichgewicht!

balance –
das Gleichgewicht

Did you **bang** your head?
Hast du dir den Kopf angeschlagen?

to bang – sich anschlagen

Don't **bang** the door!
Laß die Tür nicht so zuknallen!

to bang – zuknallen

Don't **bank on** it!
Verlaß dich nicht darauf!

to bank on – sich verlassen auf

I'll make a **bargain** with you!
Ich mache dir ein Angebot.

– *bargain*
das Angebot – offer

You drive a hard **bargain**!
Du stellst ja harte Forderungen!

– *bargain*
die Forderung – demand

It's a **bargain**!
Das ist aber günstig!

– *bargain*
günstig – reasonable

Be sensible!
Sei vernünftig!

to be – sein

Let/ him/ her/ **be**.
Laß/ ihn/ sie/ sein!

to be – sein

Be that it may.
Wie dem auch sei.

to be – sein

This problem has got me **beat**.
Mit dem Problem komme ich nicht klar.

– *beat*
klar – clear

I **beat** you to it!
Ich bin dir zuvorgekommen!

– *to beat*
zuvorkommen – to come first

BB BBB BB BBB BB BBB BB BBB BB BBB BB BBB BB BBB

Just **because**.
Weil es so ist!

because – weil

What's to **become** of you?
Was wird aus dir?

become – werden

It's **bedtime**.
Es ist Schlafenszeit.

bedtime – die Schlafenszeit

It's past your **bedtime**.
Du müßtest schon lang im Bett sein.

– bedtime
bed – das Bett

Before our very eyes!
Vor unseren eigenen Augen!

before – vor

Ladies **before** gentlemen.
Damen haben den Vortritt.

– before
der Vortritt – priority

Beggars can't be choosers.
Wer arm dran ist, kann nicht wählerisch sein.

– beggar
arm – poor

Begin at the beginning.
Fang ganz von vorn an!

to begin – anfangen

To **begin** with…
Zuerst.....

– to begin
zuerst – first of all

Behave yourself!
Benimm dich!

to behave – benehmen sich

What is **behind** this?
Was steckt dahinter?

behind – dahinter

Come out from **behind** the door.
Komm hinter der Tür hervor!

behind – hinter

BB BBB BB BBB BB BBB BB BBB BB BBB BB BBB BB BBB

You're **behind** in your homework.   behind – im Rückstand
Du bist mit deinen Hausaufgaben im Rückstand.

I don't **believe** it!   to believe – glauben
Das glaube ich nicht!

Don't you **believe** it!   to believe – glauben
Das sollst du nicht glauben!

Where does this **belong**?   to belong – hingehören
Wo gehört das hin?

Who does it **belong** to?   to belong to – gehören
Wem gehört es?

That book **belongs** to your brother.   to belong to – gehören
Das Buch gehört deinem Bruder.

Don't **bend** it!   to bend – biegen
Bieg es nicht!

That's **beside** the point.   – beside
Das ist irrelevant.   irrevelant – beside the point

You are the **best** there is.   best – am besten
Du bist am besten.

You know **best**.   best – am besten
Du weißt es am besten.

Best of all...   – best
Am allerbesten...   am allerbesten – best of all

You'll want to look your **best**.   – best
Du willst besonders gut aussehen.   gut – good

BB BBB BB BBB BB BBB BB BBB BB BBB BB BBB BB BBB

You did your **best**!(possible) — *best*
Du hast dein Möglichstes getan! möglichst — as much as possible

I'll **bet** you five dollars! to bet — wetten
Ich wette mit dir fünf Dollar!

Bet you! to bet — wetten
Mal wetten!

I wouldn't **bet** on it! — *bet*
Ich würde kein Gift darauf nehmen! das Gift — poison

You had **better** go. better — besser
Du gehst jetzt wohl besser.

You'd **better** leave. better — besser
Jetzt gehst du wohl besser.

The sooner the **better**. better — besser
Je früher, desto besser.

The faster the **better**. better — besser
Je schneller, desto besser.

All the **better**. better — besser
Um so besser.

Better and **better**. better — besser
Immer besser.

I expected **better** of you. better — Besseres
Ich habe von dir Besseres erwartet.

That's **between** you and me. between — zwischen
Das bleibt aber zwischen dir und mir.

26

BB BBB BB BBB BB BBB BB BBB BB BBB BB BBB BB BBB

That's **beyond** me.   beyond – über
Das geht über meinen Verstand.

Try to think **beyond** the immediate future.   – *beyond*
Versuch, an die weitere Zukunft zu denken.   weiter – further

You are always **bickering**!   to bicker – sich zanken
Ihr zankt euch immer!

It's your **big** day tomorrow!   big – groß
Morgen ist dein großer Tag!

That's really **big** of you! (sarcasism)   – *big*
Das ist wirklich nobel von dir!   nobel – noble

I've got a **billion** things to do!   – *billion*
Ich habe allerhand zu tun!   allerhand – all sorts of things

Bit by **bit**…   bit – das Stück
Stück für Stück…

There's not a **bite** to eat!   bite – der Bissen
Es gibt keinen Bissen zu essen!

Have a **bite** to eat.   – *bite*
Iß doch 'was.   essen – to eat

Have a **bite** to eat.   – *bite*
Willst du etwas essen.   etwas – something

Bite your tongue! (Be quiet!)   – *to bite*
Halt den Mund!   halten – to hold

Don't **bite** the hand that feeds you!   – *to bite off*
Die Hand, die dich füttert, sollst du   abschlagen – to knock off
nicht abschlagen!

27

BB BBB BB BBB BB BBB BB BBB BB BBB BB BBB BB BBB

Don't **bite** my head **off!**   *– to bite off*
Reiß mir doch nicht den Kopf ab!   <u>a</u>breißen – tear off

Don't **bite off** more than you can chew!   *– to bite off*
M<u>u</u>te dir nicht zuv<u>ie</u>l zu!   sich z<u>u</u>muten – to expect from oneself

You only have yourself to **blame (for it).**   to blame – schuld
Du bist ganz all<u>ei</u>n (dar<u>a</u>n) schuld.

Nobody is **blaming** you.   *– to blame*
Es macht dir ja n<u>ie</u>mand <u>ei</u>nen V<u>o</u>rwurf.   der V<u>o</u>rwurf – reproach

My mind went **blank.**   *– blank*
Ich h<u>a</u>tte M<u>a</u>ttscheibe.   die M<u>a</u>ttscheibe – screen

You're very **blasé.**   blasé – blas<u>ie</u>rt
Du bist sehr blas<u>ie</u>rt.

The radio is on full **blast!**   *– blast*
Das R<u>a</u>dio ist voll <u>au</u>fgedreht!   voll <u>au</u>fgedreht – fully turned up

Your hair is **bleached** by the sun.   to bleach – bl<u>ei</u>chen
Dein Haar ist von der S<u>o</u>nne gebl<u>ei</u>cht.

You look **bleary-eyed.**   bleary-eyed – verschl<u>a</u>fen
Du siehst verschl<u>a</u>fen aus.

Your nose is **bleeding.**   to bleed – bl<u>u</u>ten
D<u>ei</u>ne N<u>a</u>se bl<u>u</u>tet.

Has the **bleeding** stopped?   bleeding – die Bl<u>u</u>tung
Hat die Bl<u>u</u>tung <u>au</u>fgehört?

Bless my soul!   *– to bless*
Du m<u>ei</u>ne Güte!   die Güte – goodness

BB BBB BB BBB BB BBB BB BBB BB BBB BB BBB BB BBB

You can count your **blessings**!
Du kannst von Glück reden!

– blessings
das Glück – luck

It's like the **blind** leading the blind.
Das hieße, einen Lahmen einen Blinden führen lassen.

blind – der/ die Blinde

The TV is on the **blink** again.
Das Fernsehen ist wieder kaputt.

blink – kaputt

That man is **blocking** my view.
Der Mann versperrt mir die Sicht.

to block – versperren

My nose is **blocked** up.
Meine Nase ist völlig verstopft.

blocked – verstopft

Blood is thicker than water.
Blut ist dicker als Wasser.

blood – das Blut

I **blew** it! You **blew** it!
Ich habe es verpatzt! Du hast es verpatzt!

to blow – verpatzen

Blow on your hands! (to warm them)
Blas mal auf die Hände!

to blow – blasen

Blow me a kiss!
Wirf mir eine Kußhand zu!

– to blow
zuwerfen – to throw to

Let's **blow** bubbles!
Machen wir Seifenblasen!

– to blow
machen – to make

Don't **boast**!
Gib nicht so an!

to boast – angben

We're all in the same **boat**.
Wir sitzen alle im gleichen Boot.

boat – das Boot

29

BB BBB BB BBB BB BBB BB BBB BB BBB BB BBB BB BBB

Over my dead **body**!   *– body*
Nur über meine Leiche!   die Leiche – corpse

It **boggles** my mind!   *– boggle*
Das kann man sich kaum ausmalen!   sich ausmalen –
                                            to imagine something

I'm **boiling**!   to boil – kochen
Ich koche!

Are you **bored**?   *– bored*
Langweilst du dich?   sich langweilen – to be bored

I'm **bored** to death.   *– bored to death*
Ich langweile mich zu Tode.   sich zu Tode langweilen

Borrow your brother's shirt!   to borrow – leihen
Leih mir das Hemd von deinem Bruder!

You can't have it **both** ways!   both – beides
Beides zugleich geht nicht!

I'm sorry to **bother** you, but…   to bother – belästigen
Es tut mir leid, daß ich dich damit belästige…

Don't **bother**!   *– bother*
Nicht nötig!   nötig – necessary

Don't **bother** me!   *– bother*
Laß mich in Ruhe!   die Ruhe – peace

Don't let it **bother** you! (Don't worry.) *– bother*
Mach dir deshalb keine Sorgen!   die Sorge – worry

30

BB BBB BB BBB BB BBB BB BBB BB BBB BB BBB BB BBB

I can't be **bothered**.   – *bothered*
Das ist mir egal.   egal – all the same

We'll get to the **bottom** of this.   bottom – der Grund
Wir werden dieser Sache auf den Grund kommen.

Bounce the ball!   to bounce – springen
Laß den Ball hochspringen!

It's **bound** to happen.   – *bound*
Das muß so kommen.   müssen – must, has to

You're the **brains** of the family.   – *brains*
Du bist das Genie in der Familie.   das Genie – genius

The handle **broke** off.   to break off – abbrechen
Der Henkel ist abgebrochen.

Take a **break**!   – *break*
Mach mal eine Pause!   die Pause – pause

Give me a **break**!   – *break*
Gib mir eine Chance!   die Chance – chance

Don't hold your **breath**! (It's not good for you.) breath – der Atem
Halte den Atem nicht an!

You're out of **breath**!   breath – der Atem
Du bist außer Atem!

Don't hold your **breath**! (Sarcasm)   – *breath*
Du kannst dir wohl die Beine   stehen – to stand
in den Bauch stehen!

BB BBB BB BBB BB BBB BB BBB BB BBB BB BBB BB BBB

Take a deep **breath**!
Hol tief einmal Luft!

– breath
die Luft – air

What **brought** this on?
Was hat das verursacht?

– bring on
verursachen – to cause

You've **brought** this on yourself.
Das hast du dir selbst zuzuschreiben.

– bring on
zuschreiben – to ascribe to

Stop **brooding** over it!
Brüte nicht darüber!

to brood over – brüten

You won't **budge** an inch.
Du wirst keinen Fingerbreit nachgeben.

– budge
nachgeben – to yield

There's a **bug (virus)** going around.
Da geht eine Krankheit herum.

bug – die Krankheit

Don't let it **bug** you.
Mach dir nichts daraus.

– bug
nichts – nothing

Don't **build** up your hopes!
Mach dir keine Hoffnungen!

– build
machen – to make

Your bag is **bulging** with books!
Deine Tasche ist mit Büchern prall gefüllt!

bulging – prall

What a **bumpy** road! (road condition)
Was für eine hol(e)prige Straße!

bumpy – holperig

Bundle up!
Zieh dich warm an!

– bundle up
sich anziehen – to get dressed

Don't **burst** into the room like that!
Stürz nicht so ins Zimmer herein!

to burst into –
Hereinstürzen

It's none of your **business**!	*– business*
Das geht dich nichts an!	<u>a</u>ngehen – to concern
Mind your own **business**!	*– business*
K<u>ü</u>mmere dich um d<u>ei</u>ne <u>ei</u>genen S<u>a</u>chen!	die S<u>a</u>che – thing
You children keep me very **busy**!	busy – besch<u>ä</u>ftigt
Ihr K<u>i</u>nder h<u>a</u>ltet mich sehr besch<u>ä</u>ftigt!	
I'm **busy** doing something.	busy – besch<u>ä</u>ftigt
Ich bin mit <u>e</u>twas besch<u>ä</u>ftigt.	
Let's get **busy**!	*– busy*
An die <u>A</u>rbeit!	die <u>A</u>rbeit – work
Don't be a **busybody**.	*– busybody*
Misch dich nicht <u>ü</u>berall ein.	sich <u>ei</u>nmischen – to get involved
Anything **but** that!	*– but*
<u>A</u>lles nur das nicht!	nur – only
Do you have **butterflies** (in your stomach)?	*– butterflies*
Ist es dir ganz flau im M<u>a</u>gen?	flau – queasy
Be home **by** five!	by – bis
Sei bis fünf Uhr zu H<u>au</u>se!	
It's fine **by** me.	*– by*
Von mir aus gern.	gern – happily
By then it will be too late.	by then – bis dah<u>i</u>n
Bis dah<u>i</u>n ist es schon zu spät.	
Let **bygones** be **bygones**.	*– bygones*
Laß die Vergangenheit r<u>u</u>hen!	die Verg<u>a</u>ngenheit – the past

All aboard!
Geh an Bord, bitte!
Gay ahn bohrt, BIT-teh!

Man overboard!
Mann über Bord!
Mahn EW-behr bohrt!

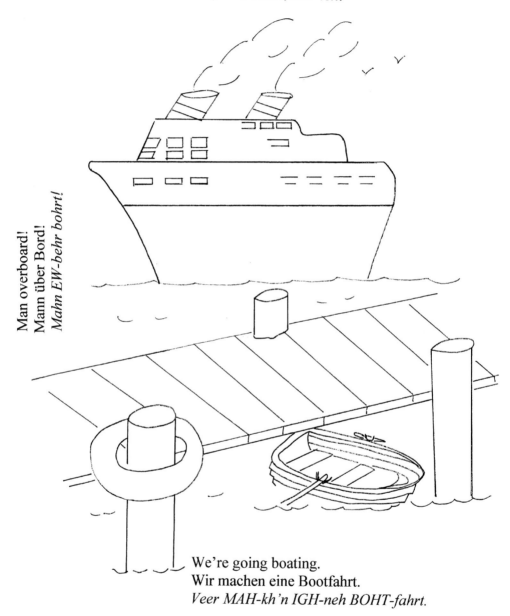

We're going boating.
Wir machen eine Bootfahrt.
Veer MAH-kh'n IGH-neh BOHT-fahrt.

C

That takes the **cake**!
Das ist ja die Höhe!

       – cake
die Höhe – height

It's a piece of **cake**! (simple)
(Es ist) ein Kinderspiel!

      – cake
das Kinderspiel – children's game

That wasn't **called for**!
Das war wirklich nicht nötig!

      – call for
nötig – necessary

Do you call that **clean**?
Das hältst du für sauber?

clean – sauber

CC CCC CC CCC CC CCC CC CCC CC CCC CC CCC CC

Can I come too?
Darf ich mitkommen?

can/ permitted – dürfen

I will do what I **can**.
Ich mache, was ich kann.

can/ able – können

You do it; I **can't**.
Mach du es; ich kann's nicht.

can/ able – können

It **can't** be done!
Das läßt sich nicht machen!

– *can*
sich lassen – allow itself

You don't have a **care** in the world.
Du hast keinerlei Sorgen.

care – die Sorge

I couldn't **care** less.
Es ist mir doch völlig egal.

– *care*
egal – all the same

I don't **care**
Das ist mir egal.

– *care*
egal – all the same

Take **care**! (Goodbye!)
Tschüs, mach's gut!

– *care*
tschüs – goodbye

It will (won't) take **care** of itself.
Das regelt sich (nicht) von selbst.

– *care*
sich regeln – to arrange itself

Don't get **carried** away.
Übertreib's nicht.

– *carried away*
übertreiben – exaggerate

I can't **carry** this.
Ich kann das nicht tragen.

to carry – tragen

Carry on! (continue)
Mach weiter!

to carry on – weitermachen

CC CCC CC CCC CC CCC CC CCC CC CCC CC CCC CC

I don't like the way you are
carrying on/ behaving.
Ich mag nicht, wie du dich benimmst.

to carry on/ behave –
sich benehmen

Just in **case**…
Im Falle eines Falles...

case – der Fall

In that **case**…
In dem Fall…

case – der Fall

As the **case** may be…
Je nachdem...

– *case*
nachdem – after

Dress **casually.**
Zieh dich leger an!

casual – leger

You and your brother, you fight
like a **cat** and dog.
Du und dein Bruder, ihr vertragt euch wie
Hund und Katze.

cat – die Katze

Don't play **cat** and mouse with me.
Spiel nicht Katz(e) und Maus mit mir!

cat – die Katze

You let the **cat** out of the bag!
Du hast die Katze aus dem Sack gelassen!

cat – die Katze

What's the **catch**?
Was ist der Haken?

catch – der Haken

Did you **catch** your finger in the drawer?
Hast du dir den Finger in der Schublade eingeklemmt?

catch – einklemmen

Don't **catch** your fingers in the door!
Laß dir die Finger nicht in der Tür einklemmen!

catch – einklemmen

37

CC CCC CC CCC CC CCC CC CCC CC CCC CC CCC CC

Don't let me **catch** you doing that again!   to catch – erwischen
Schau, daß ich dich nicht wieder dabei erwische.

We got **caught** in the rain.   *– to catch*
Wir wurden vom Regen überrascht.   überraschen – to surprise

You'll **catch** it! (get into trouble)   *– to catch*
Du wirst 'was erleben!   erleben – to experience

I'll **catch** you later!   *– to catch*
Bis später!   bis – until

I **caught** this cold.   to catch a cold – sich erkälten
Ich habe mich erkältet.

It's all in a good **cause**.   *– cause*
Es ist alles für eine gute Sache.   die Sache – thing

This calls for a **celebration**!   to celebrate – feiern
Das muß gefeiert werden!

Do you know that for **certain**?   certain – sicher
Bist du ganz sicher?

You need to **challenge** yourself.   *– to challenge*
Du mußt dir ein Ziel setzen.   das Ziel – goal

Now's your **chance**!   chance – die Chance
Das ist deine Chance!

You won't get another **chance**!   chance – die Gelegenheit
Das ist eine einmalige Gelegenheit!

Don't take any **chances**!   chance – das Risiko
Geh auf kein Risiko ein!

38

CC CCC CC CCC CC CCC CC CCC CC CCC CC CCC CC

Would you by any **chance**…   – *chance*
Könntest du vielleicht...   vielleicht – perhaps

There's no **chance** of that happening.   – *chance*
Es gibt keine Möglichkeit,   die Möglichkeit – possibility
daß es geschieht.

I won't **change** my mind.   to change – ändern
Ich werde meine Meinung nicht ändern.

Let's **change** the subject!   to change – wechseln
Wechseln wir das Thema!

Don't **change** the subject!   to change – wechseln
Wechsle nicht das Thema!

I've **changed** my mind.   – *to change*
Ich habe es mir anders überlegt.   anders – otherwise

You'd better **change** your ways!   – *to change*
Du sollst dich verbessern!   sich verbessern – improve oneself

For a change, let's eat home.   change –
Zur Abwechslung essen wir zu Hause!   die Abwechslung

Who is in **charge** here?   – *charge*
Wer ist hier der Verantwortliche?   der Verantwortliche –
                                         the responsible one

Charity begins at home.   – *charity*
Man soll zuerst an seine eigene   eigen – own
Familie denken.

You lead a **charmed** life. (lucky)   – *charmed*
Du hast einen Schutzengel!   der Schutzengel – guardian angel

39

CC CCC CC CCC CC CCC CC CCC CC CCC CC CCC CC

Three **cheers** for .....
Ein dreifaches Hurra für ....

cheer – das Hurra

Cheer up!
Laß den Kopf nicht hängen!

– *to cheer up*
hängen – to hang

Cheerio!
Tschüs!

cheerio – Tschüs

Say **cheese!** (photo-taking)
Zeig mal die Zähne!

cheese
Zähne – teeth

Don't **chicken out!**
Sei nicht feig!

– *to chicken out*
feig – cowardly

You're only a **child.**
Du bist bloß ein Kind.

child – das Kind

It's **child's** play.
Es ist ein Kinderspiel.

– *child*
das Kinderspiel – child's game

There's a **chill** in the air.
Es ist ziemlich frisch draußen.

– *chill*
frisch – cool

I'll take the **chill** off your milk.
Ich werde dir die Milch etwas
erwärmen.

– *chill*
erwärmen – warm up

Chill out! (Stay calm!)
Bleib ruhig!

– *chill out*
ruhig – calm

You have a **chip** on your shoulder.
Du hast einen Komplex.

– *chip*
der Komplex – complex

There isn't much **choice.**
Es bleibt nicht viel anderes übrig.

– *choice*
übrig – left

40

CC CCC CC CCC CC CCC CC CCC CC CCC CC CCC CC

It was an unfortunate **choice** of words.　　*– choice*
Leider hat er sich nicht gerade schön　　ausdrücken – to express
ausgedrückt.

You have no **choice** in this matter.　　*– choice*
Du hast in dieser Sache nichts zu sagen.　die Sache – thing

I'll do what I **choose.**　　*– to choose*
Ich mache, was ich will.　　wollen – to want

Don't **chop** my head off!　　*– to chop*
Das kann doch den Kopf kosten!　　kosten – to cost

The water looks **choppy.**　　choppy – kabbelig
Das Wasser sieht kabbelig aus.

Try to finish your **chores** early!　　chore – die Aufgabe
Versuch deine Aufgaben frühzeitig zu erledigen!

What a **chore!**　　chore – die Aufgabe
Was für eine Aufgabe!

You're rather **chummy** with/ him/ her/.　chummy – befreundet
Du bist mit/ ihm/ ihr/ sehr gut befreundet.

Under no **circumstances....**　　circumstances – die Umstände
Unter gar keinen Umständen....

Clean out your closet!　　to clean – saubermachen
Mach deinen Kleiderschrank gründlich sauber!

I need to **clear** it with my/ dad/ mom/.　to clear – klären
Das muß ich mit/ meinem Vater/ meiner Mutter/ klären.

41

CC CCC CC CCC CC CCC CC CCC CC CCC CC CCC CC

I'm not **clear** what you mean   clear – klar
Mir ist immer noch nicht klar,was du meinst.

Let's **clear** the air!   clear – rein
Wir sollen die Sache ins Reine bringen!

You're in the **clear**.   clear – schuldlos
Du bist schuldlos.

That **clinches** it!   *– to clinch*
Damit ist der Fall erledigt!   erledigen – to take care off

Clip these two pages together!   to clip – zusammenklemmen
Klemme diese zwei Seiten zusammen!

Everything is going like **clockwork**.   *– clockwork*
Alles läuft wie am Schnürchen.   laufen – to run

Close the door after you!   to close – zumachen
Mach die Tür hinter dir zu!

That was a **close** call!   close – knapp
Das war knapp!

You're **close** to tears!   close – nah
Du bist den Tränen nah!

You're on **cloud** nine!   *– cloud*
Du bist im siebten Himmel!   der Himmel – heaven

You have your head in the **clouds**!   *– cloud*
Du schwebst in höheren Regionen!   die Region – region

Join the **club**!   *– club*
Warum soll es dir besser gehen!   besser – better

CC CCC CC CCC CC CCC CC CCC CC CCC CC CCC CC

I **coddle** you too much.
Ich verhätschle dich zuviel.

to coddle – verhätscheln

You'll catch your death of **cold**!
Du wirst dich schrecklich erkälten!

– *cold*
sich erkälten – to catch cold

Take things as they **come**!
Nimm die Dinge, wie sie kommen!

to come – kommen

Come to the point.
Komm zur Sache!

to come – kommen

That's what **comes** of being too lazy.
Das kommt davon, wenn man zu faul ist.

to come – kommen

The string has **come** loose.
Die Schnur ist locker geworden.

– *to come*
geworden – gotten

Come what may.
Ganz gleich was passiert.

– *to come*
passieren – to happen

What **comes** next?
Was passiert jetzt?

– *to come*
passieren – to happen

Come and see me before you leave.
Schau vorbei, bevor du gehst!

– *to come*
vorbeischauen – to look by

How did the door **come** to be open?
Wieso ist die Tür geöffnet?

– *to come*
wieso – how come

Come along!
Komm mit!

to come along – mitkommen

How's the project **coming along**?
Was macht das Projekt?

– *to come along*
machen – make, do

43

CC CCC CC CCC CC CCC CC CCC CC CCC CC CCC CC

That's where you **come** in!   *– to come in*
Dann fängt deine Rolle an!   anfangen – to begin

The wheel has **come off** my wagon.   to come off –
Das Rad ist von meinem Karren   herunterkommen
heruntergekommen.

Come off it!   *– to come off*
Nun mach mal halblang!   halblang – half as long

What's c**ome over** you!   *– to come over*
Was ist denn in dich gefahren!   fahren – to travel

I don't know if I'm **coming** or going!   *– coming*
Alles kommt mir ganz   durcheinander – confusing
durcheinander vor!

We're **coming up to** Christmas.   *– coming up to*
Bald ist Weihnachten.   bald – soon

I wouldn't feel **comfortable** doing that.   *– comfortable*
Mir ist nicht ganz wohl damit!   wohl – well

You had it **coming** to you.   coming – kommen
Das mußte ja so kommen!

We're expecting **company.**   company – der Besuch
Wir erwarten Besuch.

Keep me **company**!   company – die Gesellschaft
Leiste mir Gesellschaft!

There is no **comparison**.   comparison – der Vergleich
Es gibt keinen Vergleich.

CC CCC CC CCC CC CCC CC CCC CC CCC CC CCC CC

You can **complain** till you're   to complain – sich beklagen
blue in the face!
Du kannst dich beklagen bis du rot im Gesicht anläufst.

You're always **complaining**!   to complain – sich beklagen
Du beklagst dich immer!

How are things? I can't **complain**.   to complain – sich beklagen
Wie geht's? Ich kann mich nicht beklagen!

You have cause for **complaint**.   complaint – die Klage
Du hast einen Grund, eine Klage zu führen.

It came as a **complete** surprise!   complete – völlig
Es war eine völlige Überraschung!

You have to reach a **compromise**.   compromise – der
Ihr müßt Kompromisse schließen.   Kompromiß

You have no **concept (of it)**!   concept (of it) –
Du hast (davon) keinen Begriff!   der Begriff (davon)

It's no **concern** of/ mine/ yours/.   concern – angehen
Das geht/ mich/ dich/ nichts an.

There's no cause for **concern**!   – concern
Kein Grund zur Aufregung!   die Aufregung – excitement

Don't jump to **conclusions**!   conclusion – der Schluß
Zieh keine vorschnellen Schlüsse!

On one **condition**…   condition – die Bedingung
Unter einer Bedingung (Voraussetzung)...

You're in no **condition** to go to school.   condition – die
Du bist in keiner Verfassung, zur Schule zu gehen.   Verfassung

CC CCC CC CCC CC CCC CC CCC CC CCC CC CCC CC

On the **condition** that…   condition – die Voraussetzung
(you speak to me first).
Unter der Voraussetzung, daß….. (du zuerst mit mir sprichst).

On no **condition** do you stay up late!   – condition
Auf keinen Fall bleibst du spät auf!   der Fall – case

You're **confined** to bed!   – confined
Du mußt das Bett hüten!   hüten – to keep

Consider it done!   – consider
Gesagt! Getan!   Gesagt! Getan – Said! Done!

Show some **consideration (for it)!**   consideration (for it) –
Nimm Rücksicht (darauf)!   die Rücksicht (darauf)

You **continue** to do the same thing!   – to continue
Du machst nach wie vor immer das gleiche!   nach wie vor –
                                    the same as ever

You've lost **control** of yourself!   control – die
Du hast die Selbstbeherrschung verloren!   Selbstbeherrschung

Control yourself!   to control – sich beherrschen
Beherrsch dich!

If it is **convenient** for you…   – convenient
Wenn es dir paßt,……   passen – to suit

How can I **convince** you?   to convince – überzeugen
Wie kann ich dich überzeugen?

What's/ **cooking**/ happening/?   – cooking
Was gibt's Neues?   Neues – new

CC CCC CC CCC CC CCC CC CCC CC CCC CC CCC CC

You're **cooking** up a story.
Du braust wohl eine Geschichte
zusammen!

– cooking
zusammenbrauen –
to cook up

This cold drink will **cool** you down.
Dieses kalte Getränk wird dich erfrischen.

– cool
erfrischen – to refresh

Don't lose your **cool**.
Reg dich nicht auf!

– cool
sich aufregen – to get excited

Keep a **cool** head.
Verlier nicht den Kopf!

– cool
verlieren – to lose

Cool your heels!
Warte ein bißchen!

– cool
warten – to wait

I just can't **cope**!
Ich schaffe es nicht mehr!

– cope
schaffen – to do

Do a good job! Don't cut **corners**!
Mach's gut! Kürz es nicht ab!

– corners
abkürzen – to shorten

I stand **corrected**.
Ich nehme alles zurück.

– corrected
zurücknehmen – to take back

Whatever it **costs**!
Kostet es, was es wolle!

to cost – kosten

That will **cost** a fortune!
Das wird ein Vermögen kosten!

to cost – kosten

How **could** you!
Wie konntest du!

could – konnte

That doesn't **count**.
Das zählt nicht.

to count – zählen

CC CCC CC CCC CC CCC CC CCC CC CCC CC CCC CC

Don't **count** your chickens before   – *to count*
they're hatched!   loben – to praise
Man soll den Tag nicht vor dem Abend loben!

Count yourself lucky!   – *to count*
Du bist ein Glückspilz!   der Glückspils – lucky mushroom

Do me the **courtesy** of listening.   courteous – höflich
Sei so höflich und hör mal zu!

We **covered** a lot of ground.   – *to cover*
Wir haben heute viel geschafft.   schaffen – to do

I feel **cozy**.   cozy – gemütlich
Es ist mir gemütlich.

It's **cozy** here.   cozy – gemütlich
Hier ist es gemütlich.

It's not all it's **cracked** up to be.   – *cracked*
So toll ist es dann auch wieder nicht.   toll – great

Get **cracking**!   – *cracking*
Leg los!   loslegen – get started

I have a **craving** for ice cream.   – *craving*
Ich habe Appetit auf Eis.   der Appetit – appetite, hunger

You're driving me **crazy**!   crazy – verrückt
Du machst mich verrückt!

I have to give you **credit**.   – *credit*
Das muß ich dir hoch anrechnen.   anrechnen – to credit

Where **credit's** due.   – *credit*
Ehre, wem Ehre gebührt.   die Ehre – honor

48

CC CCC CC CCC CC CCC CC CCC CC CCC CC CCC CC

Cross my heart!   *– to cross*
Ehrenwort!   das Ehrenwort – word of honor

We'll **cross** that bridge when we   *– to cross*
come to it!   zukommen – to approach
Lassen wir das Problem erst mal auf uns zukommen!

Make the sign of the **cross** like this.   to cross (oneself) –
Man bekreuzigt sich so.   sich bekreuzigen

Keep your fingers **crossed** (for me)!   *– crossed (for me)*
Drück (mir) den Daumen!   drücken – to press

That's the way the cookie **crumbles**!   *– to crumble*
Pech gehabt!   das Pech – bad luck

Give it to her before she **cries**.   to cry – weinen
Gib's ihr, bevor sie weint.

Have a good **cry**.   to cry – weinen
Weine ruhig – das wird dir guttun.

You're **crying** your eyes out!   to cry – weinen
Du weinst herzzerreißend!

It's not my **cup** of tea!   *– cup*
Das ist nicht mein Fall!   der Fall – case

Curl up on the sofa.   to curl – sich kuscheln
Kuschle dich auf das Sofa!

That is a nasty **cut**!   cut – der Schnitt
Das ist ein böser Schnitt!

Cut it out!   *– to cut*
Hör auf!   aufhören – to stop

49

TV is **cutting** into your free time.	– *to cut into*
Das Fernsehen nimmt von deiner	wegnehmen –
Freizeit weg.	to take away

You really have your work **cut** out for you.	– *cut out*
Du hast wirklich alle Hände voll zu tun.	voll – full

D

What's the **damage**?
Wieviel k_ostet der Spaß?

– damage
k_osten – to cost

Don't you **dare** lay a finger on him!
Unterst_eh dich, ihn _anzufassen!

to dare – sich unterst_ehen

Just you **dare** and see what happens!
Wenn du es w_agst, siehst du gleich, was pass_iert!

to dare – w_agen

Don't you **dare** come home late!
Wag es nicht, spät nach H_ause zu k_ommen!

to dare – w_agen

DD DDD DD DDD DD DDD DD DDD DD DDD DD DDD DD

Be a **darling**.
Sei so lieb.

— *darling*
lieb – dear, loving

It **dawned** on me that…
Es dämmerte mir.....

to dawn – sich dämmern

It's been quite a **day**!
So ein aufregender Tag!

day – der Tag

One of these **days**…
Eines Tages.....

day – der Tag

That will be the **day**!
Das möchte ich erleben!

— *day*
erleben – to experience

You make my **day**!
Du machst mir immer eine Freude!

— *day*
die Freude – joy

Any **day** now!
Irgendwann!

— *day*
irgendwann – sometime

Take a **day** off tomorrow.
Nimm morgen frei!

— *day*
morgen – tomorrow

Let's call it a **day**.
Machen wir Schluß!

— *day*
der Schluß – conclusion, finish

If Dad finds out, you're **dead**!
Wenn Vati das erfährt, dann wirst du
dein blaues Wunder erleben!

— *dead*
erleben – to experience

I am **dead set** against it!
Ich bin hundertprozentig dagegen!

— *dead set*
hundertprozentig –
one hundred percent

DD DDD DD DDD DD DDD DD DDD DD DDD DD DDD DD

It's a **deal**!
Abgemacht!

        – deal
abgemacht – it's a deal

It's no big **deal!**
Das ist keine große Sache!

      – deal
die Sache – thing

I'll **deal** with you later.
Mit dir werde ich später abrechnen!

– to deal with
abrechnen – to settle with

I know how to **deal** with it.
Ich weiß, was zu machen ist.

– to deal with
machen – to do

Do a good **deed** today!
Tu heute eine gute Tat!

deed – die Tat

No swimming in the **deep** end of the pool! deep – tief
Kein Schwimmen im tiefen Ende vom Schwimmbad!

It's not **definite** yet.
Es ist noch nicht sicher.

definite – sicher

Definitely not!
Bestimmt nicht!

definite(ly) – bestimmt

To a **degree**.
Bis zu einem bestimmten Punkt.

– degree
der Punkt – point

Don't **delay!**
Schieb es nicht hinaus!

– to delay
hinausschieben – to push off

You're a **demanding** child.
Du bist ein anspruchsvolles Kind.

demanding – anspruchsvoll--

That **depends**.
Das kommt darauf an.

to depend on – ankommen auf

DD DDD DD DDD DD DDD DD DDD DD DDD DD DDD DD

Are you **depressed**?   depressed – deprimiert
Bist du deprimiert?

You got what you **deserved**!   to deserve – verdienen
Das hast du verdient!

You'll **develop** a taste for it!   *– to develop*
Es wird dir mit der Zeit schmecken!   mit der Zeit – in time

You little **devil**!   devil – der Teufel
Du bist ein kleiner Teufel!

You ought to keep a **diary**.   diary – das Tagebuch
Du sollst ein Tagebuch führen.

I'm **dying** for a sundae!   *– to die for*
Ich würde für einen Eisbecher alles geben.   geben – to give

We have to resolve our **differences**.   difference – die
Wir müssen unsere Meinungs-   Meinungsverschiedenheit
verschiedenheiten beilegen.

That doesn't make any **difference**.   difference –
Das macht keinen Unterschied.   der Unterschied

That makes all the **difference**!   difference –
Das macht einen großen Unterschied!   der Unterschied

You just want to be **different**.   different – anders
Du willst bloß anders sein.

Things will look **different** in the morning.   different – anders
Morgen sieht alles anders aus.

DD DDD DD DDD DD DDD DD DDD DD DDD DD DDD DD

You're just being **difficult**.
Du willst nur Schwierigkeiten machen.

difficulty –
die Schwierigkeit

Dig in your heels!
Bleib standfest!

– *to dig*
standfest – steadfast

What's for/ lunch/ **dinner**/?
Was gibt's zum/ Mittagessen/ Abendessen/?

dinner – das Abendessen

Are you **disappointed**?
Bist du enttäuscht?

disappointed – enttäuscht

I can't see any sense in continuing
this **discussion**.
Ich sehe keinen Sinn, diese Besprechung fortzusetzen.

discussion –
die Besprechung

It's an absolute **disgrace**!
Das ist eine große Schande!

disgrace – die Schande

How **disgusting**!
Es ist so abstoßend!

disgusting – abstoßend

You're easily **distracted**.
Du läßt dich leicht ablenken.

to distract – ablenken

(Don't) **divide** the money between you.
Teilt (nicht) das Geld zwischen euch auf!

to divide – aufteilen

It's got to be **done**.
Das muß gemacht werden.

to do – machen

You can't always **do** just as you like.
Du kannst es nicht immer so machen,
wie du willst.

to do – machen

DD DDD DD DDD DD DDD DD DDD DD DDD DD DDD DD

How could you **do** such a thing?   to do – m<u>a</u>chen
Wie hast du so <u>e</u>twas m<u>a</u>chen k<u>ö</u>nnen?

Do exactly as you are told.   to do – m<u>a</u>chen
Mach es gen<u>au</u>, wie man es dir sagt.

It's got to be **done**.   to do – m<u>a</u>chen
Das muß gem<u>a</u>cht w<u>e</u>rden.

It just isn't **done**!   to do – m<u>a</u>chen
Das macht man <u>ei</u>nfach nicht!

We **did** it!   to do – sch<u>a</u>ffen
Wir h<u>a</u>ben es gesch<u>a</u>fft!

Don't **do** it again!   to do – tun
Tu das nicht w<u>ie</u>der!

I couldn't bring myself to **do** it.   to do – tun
Ich k<u>o</u>nnte mich nicht daz<u>u</u> br<u>i</u>ngen, es zu tun.

I would **do** anything for you.   to do – tun
Ich w<u>ü</u>rde <u>a</u>lles für dich tun.

We have a great deal to **do**.   to do – tun
Wir h<u>a</u>ben viel zu tun.

Do it this instant!   to do – tun
Tu es sof<u>o</u>rt!

I'll **do** it now!   to do – tun
Ich t<u>u</u>e es jetzt!

Do you mind not **doing** that?   to do – tun
Macht es dir 'was aus, wenn ich dich b<u>i</u>tte, das nicht w<u>ei</u>ter zu tun?

DD DDD DD DDD DD DDD DD DDD DD DDD DD DDD DD

We'll have to make **do**.
Wir müssen damit auskommen.

– to do
auskommen – to get by

This will never **do**!
Das geht nie!

– to do
gehen – to go

It will (won't) **do**.
Das geht (nicht).

– to do
gehen – to go

That'll **do**!
Das genügt!

– to do
genügen – to suffice

I want you to have nothing to **do with** him!
Ich will, daß du mit ihm nichts zu tun hast!

to do with – tun mit

You can't teach an old **dog** new tricks.
Der Mensch ist ein Gewohnheitstier.

– dog
das Gewohnheitstier –
creature of habit

Is this your **doing**?
Ist das dein Werk?

– doing
das Werk – deed, act

That takes some **doing**.
Da gehört schon etwas dazu.

– doing
gehören – to belong to

Are you in the **doldrum**s?
Bist du betrübt?

– doldrums
betrübt – saddened

Have you **done** complaining?
Bist du mit dem Schimpfen fertig?

done – fertig

What's done is **done**.
Was geschehen ist, kann man nicht
ungeschehen machen.

– done
geschehen – to happen

57

DD DDD DD DDD DD DDD DD DDD DD DDD DD DDD DD

The damage is **done**.   *– done*
Man kann es nicht wieder gutmachen.   gutmachen – to correct

Do you **doubt** me?   to doubt – anzweifeln
Willst du mich anzweifeln?

I **doubt** it.   to doubt – bezweifeln
Das bezweifle ich.

I'll give you the benefit of the **doubt**.   *– doubt*   – sich
Trotz allem verlasse ich mich auf dich.   verlassen auf – depend on

I'm **down to** my last dollar!   *– down to*
Ich bin pleite!   pleite – bankrupt

You look **dreadful**.   dreadful(ly) – schrecklich
Du siehst schrecklich aus.

It would be a **dream** come true!   dream – der Traum
Dann wäre mein Traum Wahrheit geworden!

I wouldn't **dream** of it!   dream – der Traum
Das würde mir nicht im Traum einfallen!

It worked like a **dream**!   *– dream*
Es hat hervorragend geklappt!   hervorragend – splendidly

You're in a **dream world**.   *– dreamworld*
Du lebst in einer Fantasiewelt!   die Fantasiewelt world of fantasy

You're letting things **drift**.   to drift – treiben
Du läßt die Dinge treiben.

You **drive** a hard bargain!   *– to drive*
Du stellst harte Forderungen!   stellen – to place

What are you **driving at**?　　　　to drive at – hin<u>au</u>swollen
Wor<u>au</u>f willst du hin<u>au</u>s?

Let it **drop**!　　　　　　　　　　　*– to drop*
L<u>a</u>ß es f<u>a</u>llen!　　　　　　f<u>a</u>llenlassen – to let fall

You're **dropped from** the team?　　*– to drop from*
Du bist von der M<u>a</u>nnschaft　　<u>au</u>sschließen – to exclude
<u>au</u>sgeschlossen?

I'll **drop** you at school.　　　　to drop off – <u>a</u>bsetzen
Ich s<u>e</u>tze dich an der Sch<u>u</u>le ab.

Stop **drumming** on the table!　　　to drum – tr<u>o</u>mmeln
Hör auf, mit den F<u>i</u>ngern auf den Tisch zu tr<u>o</u>mmeln!

Don't **duck out of** doing your chores!　　to duck out of –
Drück dich nicht vor d<u>ei</u>nen <u>Au</u>fgaben!　　sich dr<u>ü</u>cken vor

You're **due** an apology.　　　　*– due*
Ich sch<u>u</u>lde dir <u>ei</u>ne Entsch<u>u</u>ldigung.　　sch<u>u</u>lden – to owe

Don't act **dumb**!　　　　　　　dumb – dumm
Stell dich nicht so dumm an!

You're feeling down in the **dumps**.　　*– dumps*
Du f<u>ü</u>hlst dich am B<u>o</u>den zerst<u>ö</u>rt.　　zerst<u>ö</u>rt – destroyed

You're at bat.
Du bist dran!
Doo bihst drahn!

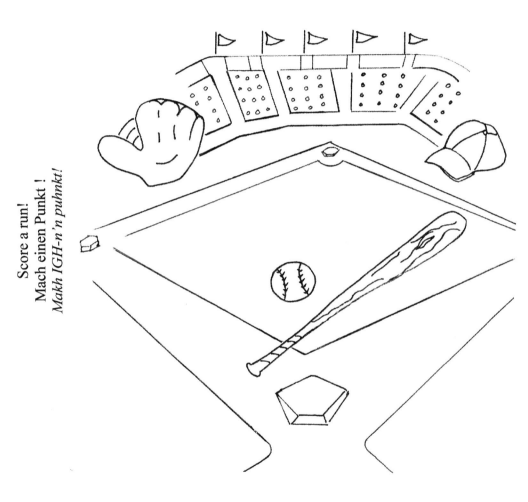

Score a run!
Mach einen Punkt !
Makh IGH-n'n puhnkt!

/Catch/ Throw/ the ball.
/Fang/Wirf/ den Ball!
/Fahng/ Veerf/ dehn Ball!

E

You're an **eager beaver**.   *eager beaver*
Du bist ein Arbeitstier.   das Arbeitstier – work animal

It just goes in one **ear** and out the other.   ear – das Ohr
Das geht zum einen Ohr hinein und
zum anderen Ohr hinaus.

I'm all **ears**!   ear – das Ohr
Ich bin ganz Ohr!

You have an **ear** for music.   *– ear*
Du hast ein musikalisches Gehör.   das Gehör – sense of hearing

61

EE EEE EE EEE EE EEE EE EEE EE EEE EE EEE EE EEE

At **ease**. (peaceful)   *ease*
Ich bin entspannt.   entspannt – relaxed

At first glance it looks **easy**.   easy – leicht
Auf den ersten Blick sieht es leicht aus.

You have an **easy** time of it.   easy – leicht
Das fällt dir leicht.

It's not all that **easy**.   easy – leicht
So leicht ist es aber nicht.

It's as **easy** as pie.   *– easy*
Es ist kinderleicht.   kinderleicht – child's play

I'm **easy**. (I don't mind.) You're **easy**.   *– easy*
Mir ist alles recht.   Dir ist alles recht.   recht – right

I'm **easy going**, and so are you.   *– easy*
Mir ist alles recht, und dir auch.   recht – right

He won't **eat** you!   to eat (animal) – fressen
Er wird dich schon nicht fressen!

If it works, I'll **eat** my hat!   to eat (animal) – fressen
Wenn es klappt, dann fresse ich meinen Besen!

Put some **effort** into it!   effort – die Mühe
Mach dir mehr Mühe!

Try to make the **effort**.   *– effort*
Versuch, dich anzustrengen!   anstrengen – to exert

Either come **or** go away!   either...or – entweder...oder
Entweder kommst du oder gehst du weg!

EE EEE EE EEE EE EEE EE EEE EE EEE EE EEE EE EEE

Put some **elbow grease** into it!
Streng dich mehr an!

– *elbow grease*
anstrengen – to exert

Young people should respect their **elders**.
Junge Leute sollen vor Älteren Respekt haben.

elders – die Älteren

Why **else**?
Warum sonst?

else – sonst

You needn't feel **embarrassed**.
Du brauchst nicht verlegen zu sein!

embarrassed – verlegen

Empty your pockets!
Leere die Taschen aus!

empty – ausleeren

Encore!
Zugabe!

encore – die Zugabe

You're your own worst **enemy**.
Du schadest dir selbst am meisten.

– *enemy*
schaden – to hurt

Save **energy**! Turn off the lights!
Spar Energie! Mach die Lichter aus!

energy – die Energie

You've been **engrossed** in
that book for an hour!
Du bist schon seit einer Stunde in das Buch vertieft!

engrossed (in) – vertieft in

That's about **enough**!
Das ist jetzt aber genug!

enough – genug

That's quite **enough** of that!
Das ist wirklich genug davon!

enough – genug

EE EEE EE EEE EE EEE EE EEE EE EEE EE EEE EE EEE

Enough said!   *– enough*
Ich will nicht mehr dazu sagen!   nicht mehr – no more

To **err** is human.   to err – irren
Irren ist menschlich.

I have to run an **errand**.   errand – die Besorgung
Ich muß eine Besorgung machen.

Can't you see the **error** of your ways?   error – der Fehler
Kannst du nicht deine Fehler einsehen?

Everything went wrong.   everything – alles
Alles ist schiefgegangen.

I'll make an **exception** this time.   exception – die Ausnahme
Diesmal mache ich eine Ausnahme.

That's a poor **excuse** for not   excuse – die Ausrede
having your homework.
Das ist eine schlechte Ausrede, warum du keine Hausarbeit hast.

I'm **exhausted**.   exhausted – erschöpft
Ich bin erschöpft.

You're making an **exhibition** of yourself. *– exhibition*
Du machst dich lächerlich.   lächerlich – ridiculous

What do you **expect** from him?   to expect – erwarten
Was erwartest du von ihm?

Don't **expect/ Expect** / the worst.   to expect – erwarten
Erwarte (nicht) das Schlechteste.

64

I **expect** your chores to be done by the time I get home. Ich erwarte, du machst deine Aufgaben bevor ich nach Hause komme.	to expect – erwarten
Do you know what's **expected** of you? Weißt du, was man von dir erwartet?	expected – erwartet
The result was better than I **expected**. Das Ergebnis war besser, als was ich erwartet habe.	expected – erwartet
I kind of **expected** this. Ich habe es irgendwie erwartet.	expected – erwartet
I know we don't see **eye** to **eye**. Ich weiß, wir stimmen nicht miteinander überein.	– eye to eye übereinstimmen – to agree
Keep your **eyes** and ears open! Halt die Augen und die Ohren offen!	eyes – die Augen
I saw it with my own **eyes**. Das habe ich mit eigenen Augen gesehen.	eyes – die Augen
It brought tears to my **eyes**. Mir sind die Tränen gekommen.	– eyes tear – die Träne

Color the bird in the color that you want.
Male den Vogel in der Farbe, die du willst.
MAH-leh dain FOH-gehl ihn dehr FAHR-beh, dee doo vilist.

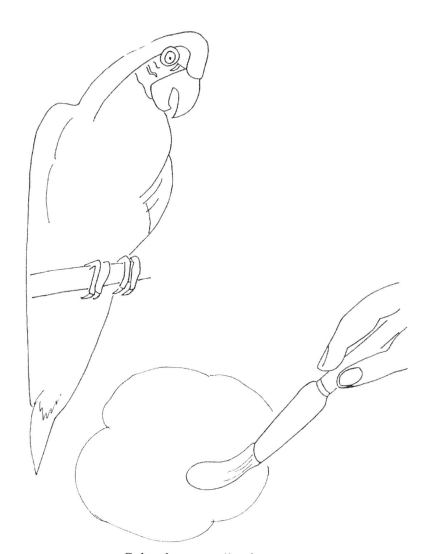

She may use the crayons!
Sie darf die Farbstifte gebrauchen!
Zee dahrf dee FAHRP-shtif-teh geh-BRAOU-sh'n!

Color the sun yellow!
Male die Sonne gelb!
MAH-leh dee ZOHN-neh gehlp!

F

Your **face** is red.
Dein Gesicht ist rot.

face – das Gesicht

Try to keep a straight **face**!
Verzieh keine Miene!

– *face*
die Miene – facial expression

Don't be afraid to lose **face**.
Hab keine Angst, dich zu blamieren!

– *face*
sich blamieren –
to embarass oneself

It's a **fact** of life.
So ist es im Leben.

– *fact*
so – so

67

FF FFF FF FFF FF FFF FF FFF FF FFF FF FFF FF FFF FF

It never **fails.**
Es kommt immer etwas Anderes
dazwischen.

– fails
dazwischenkommen –
to intervene

It's not **fair.**
Es ist nicht gerecht.

fair – gerecht

To be **fair**…
Um gerecht zu sein....

fair – gerecht

You'll get your **fair** share.
Du bekommst deinen Anteil.

– fair
der Anteil – share

Don't **fall** all to pieces!
Dreh nicht durch!

– to fall
durchdrehen – to go crazy

I'm not **falling for** that.
Darauf falle ich gar nicht herein.

to fall for – hereinfallen auf

Blonde hair runs in the **family.**
Blondes Haar liegt in der Familie.

family – die Familie

I'm not a football **fan.**
Ich bin kein Fußballfan (Fußballanhänger).

fan – der Fan, der Anhänger

Fancy meeting you here!
Wer hätte gedacht, ich treffe dich hier.

– fancy
gedacht – thought

Are you trying to pull a **fast one** on me?
Willst du mich wohl übers Ohr hauen?

– fast one
übers Ohr – over the ears

Fat chance!
Keine Chance!

– fat
keine – no

Whose **fault** is it!
Wer ist schuld?

– fault
schuld – guilty

FF FFF FF FFF FF FFF FF FFF FF FFF FF FFF FF FFF FF

It wasn't my **fault**.
Ich war nicht schuld.

– fault
schuld – guilty

May I ask you a **favor**?
Darf ich dich um einen Gefallen bitten?

favor – der Gefallen

I **fear** the worst.
Ich befürchte das Schlimmste.

to fear – befürchten

That should put the **fear** of God in you!
Das soll dir gewaltig Angst einjagen!

fear – die Angst

No **fear**!
Keine Angst!

fear – die Angst

You could have knocked me
down with a **feather**!
Ich war wie vom Donner gerührt!

– feather
der Donner – thunder

I'm getting **fed up** with your excuses.
Mir reicht's mit deinen Ausreden.

– to be fed up
reichen – to do

You'll soon get the **feel** of it.
Du wirst dich bald daran gewöhnen.

– feel
sich gewöhnen –
      to get used to

How would you **feel** if I did that?
Was hältst du davon, wenn ich das mache.

– to feel
halten von –
      to think of

I know the **feeling**!
Ich kenne das Gefühl!

feeling – das Gefühl

I had a **feeling** I might find you here.
Ich hatte das Gefühl, daß ich dich hier finde.

feeling – das Gefühl

69

FF FFF FF FFF FF FFF FF FFF FF FFF FF FFF FF FFF FF

No hard **feelings**!
Ich nehme es dir nicht übel.

– feelings
übelnehmen – to resent

Stop/ **fighting**/ quarreling/!
Hört auf mit dem Streiten!

fighting – das Streiten

This is a **film** intended for children.
Dieser Film ist für Kinder gedacht.

film – der Film

That's my **final** warning!
Das ist meine letzte Warnung!

final – letzt(e)

And that's **final**!
Und damit ist Schluß!

– final
der Schluß – end

How did you **find** the exam?
Wie hast du das Examen gefunden?

to find – finden

Find yourself something to do!
Such dir eine Beschäftigung!

– to find
suchen – look for

Keep your **fingers** crossed for me!
Drück mir die Daumen!

– finger
der Daumen – thumb

I can't quite put my **finger** on it.
Ich kann es nicht genau sagen.

– finger
sagen – to say

You didn't let me **finish**. (Speaking)
Du hast mich nicht aussprechen lassen.

– to finish
aussprechen –
finish speaking

Fire away! (Questions)
Fang mit den Fragen an!

– to fire
anfangen – to begin

That's the **first** I've heard of it!
Das ist mir ja ganz neu!

– first
neu – new

70

FF FFF FF FFF FF FFF FF FFF FF FFF FF FFF FF FFF FF

Ladies **first**!
Damen haben den Vortritt!

– first
der Vortritt – precedence

First come, first served!
Wer zuerst kommt, mahlt zuerst!

– first come
zuerst – first of all

I don't know the **first thing**
about computers.
Ich habe keinen blassen Schimmer von Computern.

– first thing
der Schimmer – glimmer

We have to get the car **fixed**.
Wir müssen das Auto reparieren lassen.

to fix – reparieren

He's an absolute **fool**!
Er ist ein großer Dummkopf!

fool – der Dummkopf

I'm all **for it**!
Ich bin ganz dafür!

for it – dafür

God **forbid**!
Gott bewahre!

– forbid
bewahren – to protect

It is absolutely **forbidden.**
Es ist ganz verboten.

forbidden – verboten

It's taking **forever**!
Das dauert ewig!

forever – ewig

Before I **forget**...
Bevor ich vergesse...

to forget – vergessen

I completely **forgot**.
Ich habe ganz vergessen.

to forget – vergessen

71

FF FFF FF FFF FF FFF FF FFF FF FFF FF FFF FF FFF FF

I'm **freezing**!   to freeze – fr<u>ie</u>ren
Ich fr<u>ie</u>re!

You gave me a **fright**!   fright – der Schreck
Du hast mir <u>ei</u>nen Schreck <u>ei</u>ngejagt!

I don't **frighten** easily.   to frighten – erschr<u>e</u>cken
Ich erschr<u>e</u>cke nicht leicht.

You're feeling **frisky** today!   – *frisky*
Du bist h<u>eu</u>te v<u>o</u>ller Energ<u>ie</u>!   die Energ<u>ie</u> – energy

Is someone making **fun** of you?   – *fun*
Macht sich j<u>e</u>mand <u>ü</u>ber dich l<u>u</u>stig? lustigmachen – make fun of

That's **funny**. (Strange)   funny – k<u>o</u>misch
The mayonnaise tastes **funny**.
Das ist k<u>o</u>misch. Die Mayonn<u>ai</u>se schmeckt k<u>o</u>misch.

Very **funny**!   funny – l<u>u</u>stig
Sehr l<u>u</u>stig!

Are you being **funny**?   – *funny*
Soll das ein Witz sein?   der Witz – joke

No **funny** business!   – *funny*
K<u>ei</u>ne D<u>u</u>mmheiten!   die D<u>u</u>mmheit – foolishness

That's a lot of **fuss** over nothing.   – *fuss*
Das ist viel Lärm <u>ü</u>ber nichts.   der Lärm – noise

Stop **fussing**!   – *fussing*
Mach k<u>ei</u>nen Krach!   der Krach – noise

FF FFF FF FFF FF FFF FF FFF FF FFF FF FFF FF FFF FF

G

Are you **gaining** weight?
Nimmst du zu?

to gain – zunehmen

Stop playing **games**!
Hör auf damit!

– *games*
aufhören – to stop

That's a stroke of **genius**!
Das ist ein genialer Einfall!

– *genius*
genial – brilliant

You're a real **gentlemen**.
Du bist ein feiner Herr!

gentleman – der Herr

73

GG GGG GG GGG GG GGG GG GGG GG GGG GG GGG

You're **getting** the hang of it!
Du bek<u>o</u>mmst den r<u>i</u>chtigen Dreh!

to get – bek<u>o</u>mmen

It **gets** me that…
Es <u>ä</u>rgert mich, daß...

– *to get*
sich <u>ä</u>rgern – to aggravate

I can't **get** the boat started.
Ich kann den B<u>oo</u>tsmotor nicht
zum L<u>au</u>fen br<u>i</u>ngen.

– *to get*
br<u>i</u>ngen – to bring

I'll **get** you for that!
Du wirst daf<u>ü</u>r b<u>ü</u>ssen.

– *to get*
b<u>ü</u>ssen – to make amends for

You'll **get** to do it tomorrow.
Du kannst es m<u>o</u>rgen m<u>a</u>chen.

– *to get*
k<u>ö</u>nnen – to be able, can

Why don't you **get** your sister to do it?
Warum läßt du das nicht von d<u>ei</u>ner
Schw<u>e</u>ster m<u>a</u>chen?

– *to get*
lassen – to let

I don't **get** it!
Da k<u>o</u>mme ich nicht mit!

– *to get*
m<u>i</u>tkommen – to be beyond

How well you're **getting along
with** your sister!
Wie gut vertr<u>ä</u>gst du dich mit d<u>ei</u>ner Schw<u>e</u>ster!

to get along with –
vertr<u>a</u>gen

Why aren't you **getting along
with** your brother?
Warum vertr<u>ä</u>gst du dich nicht mit d<u>ei</u>nem Br<u>u</u>der?

to get along with –
vertr<u>a</u>gen

When will you **get around to**
mowing the lawn?
Wann kommst du daz<u>u</u>, den R<u>a</u>sen zu m<u>ä</u>hen?

to get around to –
daz<u>u</u>kommen

74

GG GGG GG GGG GG GGG GG GGG GG GGG GG GGG

How do you **get away with**   – *to get away with*
talking to me like that?   erl<u>au</u>ben – to allow
Wie kannst du es dir erl<u>au</u>ben, so mit mir zu spr<u>e</u>chen?

You **get away with** murder!   – *to get away with*
Du kannst dir <u>a</u>lles erl<u>au</u>ben!   erl<u>au</u>ben – to allow

You have to **get by with** your allowance.   to get by with –
Du mußt mit d<u>ei</u>nem T<u>a</u>schengeld   <u>au</u>skommen mit
<u>au</u>skommen.

Let's **get down to** work!   – *to get down to*
M<u>a</u>chen wir uns an die <u>A</u>rbeit!   m<u>a</u>chen – to do

Don't **get into** trouble!   to get into – ger<u>a</u>ten
Ger<u>a</u>te nicht in Schw<u>ie</u>rigkeiten!

What's **got into** you?   – *to get into*
Was ist bloß in dich gef<u>a</u>hren?   f<u>a</u>hren – to drive, travel

It's time to **get** you **off** to school.   – *to get off*
Es ist Zeit, dich in die Sch<u>u</u>le zu   sch<u>i</u>cken – to send
sch<u>i</u>cken.

You've **gotten off to** a/ good/ bad/ start.   – *to get off to*
Du hast <u>ei</u>nen/ g<u>u</u>ten/ schlechten/   m<u>a</u>chen – to make
<u>A</u>nfang gem<u>a</u>cht.

You're **getting out of hand**.   – *to get out of hand*
Du gerätst <u>au</u>ßer Rand und Band!   ger<u>a</u>ten – to get

You're talking **gibberish**!   gibberisch –
Du sprichst K<u>au</u>derwelsch!   K<u>au</u>derwelsch

You're having a fit of the **giggles**!   – *giggles*
Du kannst nicht <u>au</u>fhören zu k<u>i</u>chern!   k<u>i</u>chern – to giggle

GG GGG GG GGG GG GGG GG GGG GG GGG GG GGG

That's my **girl**! (Well done!)   girl – das M<u>ä</u>dchen
M<u>ä</u>dchen, das hast du gut gem<u>a</u>cht!

I'm **glad** to help you.   *– to be glad*
Es freut mich, daß ich dir h<u>e</u>lfen kann.   fr<u>eu</u>en – to please

You look **gloomy**.   gloomy – tr<u>ü</u>bsinnig
Du siehst tr<u>ü</u>bsinnig aus.

You may as well **go**.   to go – g<u>e</u>hen
Du kannst dann r<u>u</u>hig g<u>e</u>hen.

That music will have to **go**!   *– to go*
Die Mus<u>i</u>k muß <u>a</u>bgeschafft w<u>e</u>rden!   <u>a</u>bschaffen –
                                                   to do away with

Off you **go**!   *– to go*
Fort mit dir!   fort – away

What I say **goes**! (I'm the boss here!)   *– to go*
Was ich s<u>a</u>ge, gilt!   g<u>e</u>lten – to be valid

Will you **go away**!   to go away – g<u>e</u>hen
W<u>ü</u>rdest du b<u>i</u>tte g<u>e</u>hen!

The bicycle won't **go through** the door.   *– to go through*
Das F<u>a</u>hrrad paßt nicht durch die Tür.   p<u>a</u>ssen – to fit

Can somebody tell me what is **going on**?   to go on – v<u>o</u>rgehen
Kann j<u>e</u>mand mir erkl<u>ä</u>ren, was hier v<u>o</u>rgeht?

The fuse is **going**.   *– to (be) go(ing)*
Die Z<u>ü</u>ndschnur brennt.   br<u>e</u>nnen – to burn

Exercise is **good** for you.　　　　　　good – gut
Gymnastik ist gut für dich.

So far so **good**.　　　　　　　　　good – gut
So weit, so gut.

No **good** will come of it.　　　　　good – das Gute
Nichts Gutes kommt davon.

A lot of **good** that will do!　　　　 *– good*
Das hilft dir auch nicht viel!　　　　viel – much

It's **as good as** it comes.　　　　 *– as good as*
Besser kann es nicht werden.　　　　besser – better

You'll have to **grab** the bull　　　 to grab – packen
by the horns.
Du mußt den Stier bei den Hörnern packen.

Do that again and I'll **ground** you!　　 *– to ground*
Machst du das wieder, dann kriegst　der Hausarrest – detention
du Hausarrest!

Go/outside/ inside/ and play.
Geh /nach draussen/ ins Haus hinein/ und spiele.
Geh/nakh DRAOU-z'n/ins haous hih-NIGHN/ unt SHPEEL-eh.

Play/ in the yard/ in the sand box/.
Spiel/ im Garten/ im Sandkasten/.
Shpeel / im GAHR-t'n/ eehm SAHNT-kahs-t'n/.

Don't leave the yard.
Verlasse den Garten nicht!
Fehr-LAHS-seh dain GAHR-t'n nihsht!

H

Your **hair** needs cutting.
Dein Haar muß geschnitten werden.

hair – das Haar

Don't do it **half** way!
Mach nicht nur die Hälfte!

half – die Hälfte

What actually **happened**?
Was ist eigentlich passiert?

to happen – passieren

How else do you think it **happened**?
Wie ist es sonst passiert, meinst du?

to happen – passieren

79

HH HHH HH HHH HH HHH HH HHH HH HHH HH HHH

What **happens** if…?
Was passiert, wenn....?

to happen – pass<u>ie</u>ren

Did you have a **hand** in this?
War d<u>ei</u>ne Hand auch mit im Spiel?

hand – die Hand

Don't put your **hands** in your pockets!
Steck die H<u>ä</u>nde nicht in die T<u>a</u>schen!

hands – die H<u>ä</u>nde

Hands off!
Hände weg!

hands – die H<u>ä</u>nde

Keep your **hands** off that!
Laß die F<u>i</u>nger dav<u>o</u>n!

– *hands*
die F<u>i</u>nger – fingers

Keep your **hands** off me!
Laß die F<u>i</u>nger von mir!

– *hands*
die F<u>i</u>nger – fingers

I'd **hang on to** that money , if I were you.
Ich würde an d<u>ei</u>ner St<u>e</u>lle das Geld
beh<u>a</u>lten.

– *to hang on to*
beh<u>a</u>lten – to keep

Don't **hang up**!/ **Hang up**! (telephone)
Leg (nicht) auf!

to hang up – <u>au</u>flegen

You make me **happy**.
Du machst mich gl<u>ü</u>cklich.

happy – gl<u>ü</u>cklich

You're pretty **happy-go-lucky** today!
Du bist h<u>eu</u>te ziemlich <u>u</u>nbekümmert!

happy-go-lucky –
<u>U</u>nbekümmert

I'm **hard at work**.
Ich <u>a</u>rbeite schwer.

– *hard at work*
schwer – hard

80

HH HHH HH HHH HH HHH HH HHH HH HHH HH HHH

Why are you giving me a **hard time**?
Warum machst du mir Schwierigkeiten?

– hard time
die Schwierigkeiten –
difficulties

You are **hard to please**.
Du bist schwer zufriedenzustellen.

– hard to please
schwer – hard

Do you have to learn the **hard way**?
Mußt du das auf schwierige Art lernen?

– hard way
schwierig – difficult

I see no **harm** in it.
Ich finde, es kann nicht schaden

– harm
schaden – to harm

Don't **hassle** me!
Ärgere mich nicht!

to hassle – ärgern

It's too much of a **hassle**.
Das ist zu umständlich.

– hassle
umständlich – awkward

You don't/ **have**/ stand/ a chance!
Du hast keine Chance!

to have – haben

What does that **have** to do with it?
Was hat das damit zu tun?

to have – haben

Here's what you **have** to do.
Das mußt du machen.

to have to – müssen

You **have** it in for me.
Alles, was du machst, ist gegen mich!

– to have
gegen – against

You have a good **head** for numbers.
Du hast einen Kopf für Zahlen.

head – der Kopf

Hold your **head** high!
Kopf hoch!

head – der Kopf

81

HH HHH HH HHH HH HHH HH HHH HH HHH HH HHH

I lost my **head**!   head – der Kopf
Ich habe den Kopf verloren!

Off the top of my head, I don't know.   – *off the top of my head*
Mein erster Gedanke ist, ich weiß nicht.   der Gedanke – thought

You're **heading for** trouble!   – *to be heading for*
Du bist auf dem besten Weg, Ärger   der Weg – way
zu bekommen.

We've got **heaps** of time.   – *heaps*
Wir haben sehr viel Zeit.   viel – a lot of

Can you **hear** me?   to hear – hören
Kannst du mich hören?

I won't **hear** of it!   to hear – hören
Ich will davon nichts hören!

Your **heart's** in the right place.   heart – das Herz
Du hast das Herz auf dem rechten Fleck.

You had your **heart** set on it.   heart – das Herz
Du hast dein Herz daran gehängt.

I didn't have the **heart** to tell you.   heart – das Herz
Ich konnte es nicht übers Herz bringen, es dir zu sagen.

Have a **heart**!   heart – das Herz
Gib deinem Herzen einen Stoß!

Try and **help** me!   to help – helfen
Versuch, mir zu helfen!

We always **help** one another.   to help – helfen
Wir helfen uns immer gegenseitig.

82

HH HHH HH HHH HH HHH HH HHH HH HHH HH HHH

It can't be **helped**.
So ist es!

– to be helped
so – that's the way

You've been very **helpful**.
Du warst mir sehr behilflich.

helpful – behilflich

I'll give you a **hint**.
Ich gebe dir einen Hinweis.

hint – der Hinweis

Are you **holding** something **back**?
Hältst du etwas zurück?

to hold back –
zurückhalten

Hold tight!
Halte fest!

to hold tight – festhalten

It pays to be **honest**.
Es zahlt sich heraus, ehrlich zu sein.

honest – ehrlich

I don't think you were being **honest**
with me.
Ich glaube nicht, daß du mit mir ehrlich warst.

honest – ehrlich

To be **honest**, I don't know.
Ehrlich gesagt, weiß ich nicht.

honest – ehrlich

Honesty is the best policy.
Ehrlich währt am längsten.

– honesty
ehrlich – honest

We can only **hope** for the best.
Wir können nur das Beste hoffen.

to hope – hoffen

I **hope** for the best.
Ich hoffe das Beste.

to hope – hoffen

Don't get your **hopes up**!
Erwarte nicht zuviel!

– (to get) hopes up
erwarten – to expect

83

Don't get up on your high **horse**!   horse – das Pferd
Setz dich nicht aufs hohe Pferd!

Hold your **horses**!   *– horses*
Keine Übereilung!   die Übereilung – rush

You're in a lot of **hot water**!   *– hot water*
Du bist in der Klemme!   die Klemme – fix

Tell me **how** you did it!   how – wie
Sag mir nur, wie du das geschafft hast!

How's the hand?   how – wie
Wie ist die Hand?

Get dressed in a **hurry**!   *– hurry*
Beeil dich beim Anziehen!   sich beeilen – to hurry

What's the **hurry**?   *– hurry*
Warum so eilig?   eilig – hasty

You won't do that again in a **hurry**!   *– hurry*
Das machst du so schnell nicht wieder!   schnell – fast

It wouldn't **hurt** you to wait.   to hurt – schaden
Es schadet dir nicht zu warten.

It's all right. I'm not going to **hurt** you.   to hurt – wehtun
Alles in Ordnung. Ich tue dir nicht weh.

I

I don't have the foggiest **idea**!
Ich habe keine blasse Ahnung!

idea – die Ahnung

It wasn't my **idea**!
Das war nicht meine Idee!

idea – die Idee

What put that **idea** in your head?
Wie bist du auf diese Idee gekommen?

idea – die Idee

Don't put any **ideas** in my head!
Setz mir keinen Floh ins Ohr!

idea –
der Floh – flea

85

Can you give me an **idea** how much   *idea –*
it will cost?   sagen – to say
Kannst du mir ungefähr sagen, wieviel das kosten wird?

That's a big "**if**"!   *– if*
Das ist die große Frage!   die Frage – question

If and when...   *– if and when*
Sollte ich....   sollen – should

That's **iffy**.   *– iffy*
Das ist fraglich.   fraglich – questionable

You're the **image** of your father.   image – das Ebenbild
Du bist das Ebenbild von deinem Vater.

You must have **imagined** it.   to imagine – sich einbilden
Das hast du dir nur eingebildet.

I am getting **impatient** with you.   impatient – ungeduldig
Ich werde mit dir ungeduldig.

It's of no great **importance**.   *– importance*
Das ist nicht besonders wichtig.   wichtig – important

I'm not asking **the impossible**!   (the) impossible – das
Ich verlange nicht das Unmögliche!   Unmögliche

You're **impossible**!   impossible – unmöglich
Du bist unmöglich!

It's an **impossibility**!   *– impossibility*
Das ist unmöglich!   unmöglich – impossible

I was under the **impression** that you... impression – der Eindruck
Ich hatte den Eindruck, daß du .....

86

There is room for **improvement**.
Das könnte um eigenes besser sein.

improvement–
besser – better

Inch by **inch**…
Zentimeter um Zentimeter....

– inch
der Zentimeter – centimeter

He's a/ good/ bad/ **influence** on you.
Er hat einen/ guten/ schlechten/ Einfluß auf dich.

influence – der Einfluß

Keep me **informed** (of what is happening)!
Halte mich informiert (über das, was passiert)!

informed – informiert

I had (an) (no) **inkling** of what
you were up to.
Ich hatte nicht die geringste Ahnung, was du vorhattest.

– inkling
die Ahnung – the idea

Your shirt is **inside out**.
Dein Hemd ist verkehrt herum.

– inside out
verkehrt – wrong

Must you **insist** on playing the drums!
Mußt du unbedingt trommeln!

– to insist
unbedingt – absolutely

You always **insist** on playing the drums!
Du bestehst immer darauf zu trommeln!

to insist (on) –
   bestehen (auf)

You **inspire** confidence.
Du erfüllst mich mit Vertrauen.

– to inspire
erfüllen – to fill

Do it now **instead of** talking!
Tu es jetzt statt zu reden!

instead of – statt

I have an **instinct** for this.
Ich habe ein Instinkt dafür.

instinct – das Instinkt

87

I didn't **intend** you to see it yet.
Ich hatte nicht beabsichtigt,
daß du es schon siehst.

to intend – beabsichtigen

Was that **intended**?
War das absichtlich?

intended – absichtlich

It was **intended** as a joke.
Das war als Witz gemeint.

intended – gemeint

It's in your **interest** to do it.
Das liegt in deinem eigenen Interesse,
es zu tun.

(the) interest – das
Interesse

Please, don't **interrupt** us!
Bitte, stör uns nicht

to interrupt – stören

I hope I'm not **intruding**.
Ich hoffe, ich störe nicht.

to intrude – stören

This doesn't **involve** you.
Das betrifft dich nicht.

to involve – betreffen

I was **irked** by your attitude.
Deine Einstellung hat mich geärgert.

to irk – ärgern

My arm **itches**.
Mein Arm juckt.

to itch – jucken

J

The door is **jammed**.
Die Tür klemmt.

– jammed
klemmen – to stick

You did a good **job.**
Das hast du gut gemacht.

– job
machen – to do

May I **join** you?
Darf ich mich anschließen?

to join – anschließen

Did someone play a **joke** on you?
Hat dir jemand einen Streich gespielt?

joke – der Streich

JJ JJJ JJ JJJ JJ JJJ JJ JJJ JJ JJJ JJ JJJ JJ JJJ JJ JJJ JJ JJJ JJ JJJ

It's no **joke**! I was only **joking**.   joke – der Witz
Das ist kein Witz! Das war bloß ein Witz

You're always cracking **jokes**.   jokes – die Witze
Du reißt ständig Witze.

You can't take a **joke**.   *– joke*
Du verstehst keinen Spaß.   der Spaß – fun

Don't **joke** about this!   *– to joke*
Mach doch keine Witze darüber!   der Witz – joke

You're a **joy** to be with.   *– joy*
Jeder freut sich, bei dir zu sein.   sich freuen – to be happy

I will be the **judge** of that.   to judge – beurteilen
Ich werde das selbst beurteilen.

That shows poor **judgemen**t.   judgement – das Urteilsver mögen
Das zeigt ein schlechtes Urteilsvermögen.

Against my better **judgement**….   *– judgement*
Gegen meine Überzeugung....   die Überzeugung – conviction

Don't **jump** down my throat!   *– to jump*
Fahr mich nicht an!   anfahren – to jump at

You **jump** from one thing to another!   *– to jump*
Du bleibst nie bei einer Sache!   bleiben – to stay

Why are you so **jumpy**?   *– jumpy*
Warum bist du so nervös?   nervös – nervous

I was **just about** to fix dinner.   just about – gerade
Ich wollte gerade das Abendessen richten.

JJ JJJ JJ JJJ JJ JJJ JJ JJJ JJ JJJ JJ JJJ JJ JJJ JJ JJJ JJ JJJ JJ JJJ

K

Keep your voice **down**!
Sprich bitte l<u>ei</u>se!

– to keep down
l<u>ei</u>se – quietly

I can't **keep** my food **down**.
Ich kann das <u>E</u>ssen nicht bei mir beh<u>a</u>lten.

– to keep down
beh<u>a</u>lten – to keep

I've decided to **keep** you **in**.
Ich h<u>a</u>be mich entschl<u>o</u>ssen, daß
du im H<u>au</u>se bl<u>ei</u>ben sollst.

– to keep in
im Hause – in the house

It seems to me that you are **keeping
to yourself**.
Es scheint mir, du willst für dich all<u>ei</u>ne bl<u>ei</u>ben.

– to keep to oneself
bl<u>ei</u>ben – to keep

KK KKK KK KKK KK KKK KK KKK KK KKK KK KKK

What **kept** you?
Was hat dich <u>au</u>fgehalten?

to keep, delay – <u>au</u>fhalten

Keep it up!
Mach w<u>ei</u>ter so!

to keep up – <u>wei</u>termachen

Keep up the good work!
Mach mit der g<u>u</u>ten <u>A</u>rbeit w<u>ei</u>ter!

to keep up – <u>wei</u>termachen

For keeps!
Für <u>i</u>mmer!

(for) keeps – für <u>i</u>mmer

You're just **killing** time.
Du schlägst bloß die Zeit tot.

to kill – t<u>o</u>tschlagen

Don't **kill yourself**! (someone
not working.)
Reiß dir kein Bein aus!

– to kill oneself
<u>au</u>sreißen – to tear out

Give me a **kiss** goodnight!
Gib mir <u>ei</u>nen Gute-Nacht-Kuß!

kiss – der Kuß

I **know** what's best for you.
Ich weiß, was für dich das B<u>e</u>ste ist.

to know – w<u>i</u>ssen

You **know** best!
Du weißt alles b<u>e</u>sser!

to know – w<u>i</u>ssen

You **know** your own mind.
Du weißt, was du willst.

to know – w<u>i</u>ssen

I want you to **know**.
Ich will, daß du (es) weißt.

to know – w<u>i</u>ssen

How should I **know** (that)?
Wie soll ich (das) w<u>i</u>ssen?

to know – w<u>i</u>ssen

The more I **know** about this
the/ less/ more/ I like it.   to know – wissen
Je mehr ich davon weiß, desto/ weniger/ mehr/ gefällt es mir.

As far as I **know**...   to know – wissen
Soweit ich weiß...

Heaven **knows**!   to know – wissen
Das weiß nur der Himmel!

You never **know**...   to know – wissen
Man kann nie wissen...

I'll let you **know** if...   to know – wissen
Ich lasse dich wissen, wenn...

You can never **know** too much.   – *to know*
Man lernt nie aus.   auslernen – to finish learning

You **know** right from wrong.   – *to know*
Du kannst Gut und Böse   unterscheiden – to distinguish
unterscheiden.

You should **know** better than that!   – *to know*
Du sollst mehr Verstand haben!   der Verstand – understanding

If I had only **known** (that)!   known – gewußt
Wenn ich das bloß gewußt hätte!   (p.p. of wissen)

I'm loading my truck with sand.
Ich lade meinen Lastwagen mit Sand.
Ihsh LAH-deh MIGH-n'n LAHST-vah-g'n miht zahnt.

Why don't you watch the birds?
Warum schaust du dir die Vögel nicht an?
Vah-RUHM shaoust doo dihr dee FEHR-gell nihsht ahn?

Have fun! Enjoy yourself!
Viel Spass ! Viel Vergnügen!
Feel shpahs! Feel fehrk-NEWH-g'n!

L

Poor **lamb**!
Armes Ding!

– *lamb*
das Ding – thing

This is your **last** chance!
Das ist deine letzte Chance!

last – letzt(e)

Do you have to have the **last** word?
Mußt du immer das letzte Wort haben?

last – letzt(e)

That's the **last** thing I would do!
Das ist das letzte, was ich machen würde!

(the) last – das letzte

95

LLL LL LLL LL LLL LL LLL LL LLL LL LLL LL LLL LL

It's too good to **last**.   *– to last*
Das ist zu schön, um wahr zu sein.   wahr – true

Don't stay out **late**!   late – spät
Komm nicht zu spät heim!

Don't make me **laugh**!   to laugh – lachen
Daß ich nicht lache!

It's the **law**.   law – das Gesetz
Es ist das Gesetz.

It's the **least** you can do.   (the) least – das wenigste
Es ist das wenigste, was man tun kann.

That's the **least** of my worries.   (the) least – am wenigsten
Das macht mir am wenigsten Sorgen.

You **left** the door open.   to leave – lassen
Du hast die Tür offen gelassen.

Leave it to me!   to leave – lassen
Laß mich nur machen!

Let's **leave** it at that!   to leave – lassen
Lassen wir es dabei!

I think we should **leave** it alone.   to leave – lassen
Ich meine, wir sollen es in Ruhe lassen.

Who **left** the milk out (on the table)?   to leave (standing) –
Wer hat die Milch (auf dem Tisch)   stehenlassen
stehenlassen?

Shake a **leg**!   *– leg*
Beeil dich!   sich beeilen – to hurry

LLL LL LLL LL LLL LL LLL LL LLL LL LLL LL LLL LL

The **less** said about it the better.   less – weniger
Je weniger man darüber spricht, desto besser.

I don't think any **less** of you.   less – weniger
Ich halte nicht weniger von dir.

That will teach you a **lesson**.   lesson – die Lehre
Das wird dir eine Lehre sein.

Let me do it!   to let – lassen
Laß mich es tun!

Let it pass!   to let – lassen
Laß es sein!

Don't **let** it get you down.   to let – lassen
Laß dich deswegen nicht niederdrücken!

Relax and **let off steam**!   to let off steam –
Beruhige dich und laß Dampf ab!   Dampf ablassen

What are you **letting** yourself in for?   – to *let oneself in for*
Worauf läßt du dich ein?   sich einlassen – to get involved in

Take the lid off (the plan)!   – *(to take the) lid off*
Deck den Plan ab!   abdecken – to uncover

What a **life**!   life – das Leben
Was für ein Leben!

Such is **life**!   life – das Leben
So ist das Leben!

It makes **life** worth living.   life – das Leben
So lohnt sich das Leben.

97

LLL LL LLL LL LLL LL LLL LL LLL LL LLL LL LLL LL LLL LL

Not on your **life**!
Ich bin doch nicht verrückt!

– life
verrückt – crazy

You won't **lift** a finger to help!
Du rührst keinen Finger, um zu helfen!

– to lift
rühren – to move

You really give me a **lift**.
Du munterst mich viel auf!

– lift
aufmuntern – to cheer up

I don't care whether you **like**/
he **likes**/ it or not.
Mir ist egal, ob es/ dir/ ihm/ gefällt oder nicht.

– to like
gefallen – to please

Well, I **like** that! (pleased)
Na ja, es gefällt mir!

– to like
gefallen – to please

I would **like** nothing better.
Nichts würde mir besser gefallen.

– to like
gefallen – to please

I don't **like** it at all.
Das gefällt mir überhaupt nicht!

– to like
gefallen – to please

You'll get to **like** it.
Du wirst mit der Zeit daran Gefallen
finden.

– to like
der Gefallen – pleasure

You're **like** your father.
Du bist deinem Vater ähnlich.

like – ähnlich

That's just **like** you!
Das sieht dir ähnlich!

like – ähnlich

That's more **like** it!
So ist es schon besser!

– like
besser – better

LLL LL LLL LL LLL LL LLL LL LLL LL LLL LL LLL LL

Don't be **like** that!
Sei nicht so!

like – so

Like father **like** son.
Der <u>A</u>pfel fällt nicht weit vom Stamm.

– *like...like*
f<u>a</u>llen – to fall

It's not very **likely**.
H<u>ö</u>chstwahrscheinlich pass<u>ie</u>rt es nicht!

likely – h<u>ö</u>chstwahrscheinlich

Is it to your **liking**?
Ist das zu d<u>ei</u>nem Geschm<u>a</u>ck?

– *liking*
der Geschm<u>a</u>ck – taste

You've certainly **taken a liking to** music!
Du hast eine V<u>o</u>rliebe für Mus<u>i</u>k
bek<u>o</u>mmen.

– *to take a liking to*
die V<u>o</u>rliebe – preference

You just refuse to **listen**!
Du w<u>ei</u>gerst dich <u>ei</u>nfach, z<u>u</u>zuhören!

to listen – z<u>u</u>hören

You wouldn't **listen**.
Du w<u>ü</u>rdest nicht z<u>u</u>hören.

to listen – z<u>u</u>hören

Little did I think that…
Ich h<u>ä</u>tte kaum ged<u>a</u>cht, daß...

– *little*
kaum – hardly

As long as I **live**…!
Sol<u>a</u>ng ich l<u>e</u>be...!

to live – l<u>e</u>ben

Live and let **live**.
L<u>e</u>ben und l<u>e</u>ben l<u>a</u>ssen.

to live – l<u>e</u>ben

You **live** and learn!
Man lernt nie aus!

– *to live*
<u>au</u>slernen – to stop learning

I feel **lonely**.
Ich f<u>ü</u>hle mich <u>ei</u>nsam.

lonely – <u>ei</u>nsam

99

LLL LL LLL LL LLL LL LLL LL LLL LL LLL LL LLL LL

It won't take **long**.
Es dauert nicht lang.

long – lang

I would think **long and hard** about it.
Das würde ich mich zweimal überlegen.

– *long and hard*
zweimal – twice

I don't **look** at it like that.
So betrachte ich die Sache nicht.

– *to look*
betrachten – to observe

Look on the bright side!
Sei zuversichtlich!

– *to look*
sein – to be

Look me straight in the eye!
Sieh mir direkt in die Augen!

– *to look*
to see – sehen

Look before you leap!
Erst wägen, dann wagen!

– *to look*
wägen – to consider

Let me have a **look**!
Laß mich sehen!

– *look*
to see – sehen

Have you **looked** everywhere?
Hast du überall gesucht?

to look (for) – suchen

No matter where I **look for** it,
I can't find it.
Egal, wo ich suche, ich finde es nicht.

to look for – suchen

I'm **looking forward to** your birthday.
Ich freue mich auf deinen Geburtstag.

to look forward to –
sich freuen auf

I was **looking forward to** a good game!
Ich hatte mich auf ein gutes Spiel gefreut!

to look forward to –
sich freuen auf

You **look like** your mother.
Du siehst deiner Mutter sehr ähnlich.

to look like –
ähnlich sehen

100

LLL LL LLL LL LLL LL LLL LL LLL LL LLL LL LLL LL

You **look like** you have not slept well.
Du siehst aus, als ob du nicht gut geschlafen hast.

to look like –
aussehen, als ob

Let's have a **look through** some magaizines.
Sehen wir uns ein paar Zeitschriften durch!

to look through –
durchsehen

I don't like the **looks** of this.
Das gefällt mir nicht.

– *looks*
gefallen – to please

The boat has come **loose**.
Das Boot hat sich los gemacht.

loose – los

I can't let you **loose** in the book store!
Ich kann dich in der Buchhandlung nicht
frei herumlaufen lassen.

– *loose*
frei – free(ly)

Are you **losing** interest in soccer?
Verlierst du das Interesse am Fußball?

to lose – verlieren

You've **lost** me (I don't understand)!
Ich habe den Faden verloren!

to lose – verlieren

It's no great **loss**!
Das ist kein großer Verlust!

loss – der Verlust

You're never at a **loss** for an answer!
Du bist nie eine Antwort schuldig!

– *loss*
schuldig – guilty

You've been **lost** in that book for an hour!
Du bist seit einer Stunde in das Buch vertieft!

– *to be lost in*
vertieft – engrossed

Don't push your **luck**!
Treib's nicht zu weit!

– *luck*
treiben – to push

Just your/ my **luck**!	*– luck*
Pech gehabt, wie immer!	das Pech – bad luck
It's not your **lucky** day!	*– lucky*
Heute ist wohl nicht dein Glückstag	das Glück – (good) luck
You should be so **lucky**!	*– lucky*
Du sollst auch soviel Glück haben!	das Glück – (good) luck
Don't shout at the top of your **lungs**!	*– lungs*
Schrei nicht so aus Leibeskräften!	die Leibeskräfte – full body strength

M

I'm not **made** of money!
Ich bin doch kein Krösus!

          – made
     Krösus – Crosus

You **made** my day!
Das hat mich unheimlich gefreut!

          – made
freuen – to make happy

It doesn't **make** any difference.
Das macht keinen Unterschied.

    to make – machen

Don't **make** any trouble!
Mach keinen Ärger!

    to make – machen

MM MMM MM MMM MM MMM MM MMM MM MMM

Make believe you're the "mom"!   *– to make believe*
Tu so, als ob du die Mutti bist!   tun so, als ob – to do as if

You're **making me hungry**!   to make hungry – hungrig
Du machst mich hungrig!   machen

Don't **make me laugh**!   *– to make laugh*
Bring mich nicht zum Lachen!   lachen – to laugh

I don't know what to **make**   to make of – halten von
of that remark.
Ich weiß nicht, was ich von der Bemerkung halten soll.

You **make me sad**.   to make sad – traurig machen
Du machst mich traurig.

Dad and I want you to **make**   *– to make something of yourself*
something of yourself.   der Erfolg – success
Vater und ich wollen, daß du im Leben Erfolg hast.

Make up your mind!   to make up/ decide – sich entschließen
Entschließ dich!

Make up, and give each other a kiss!   to make up –
Versöhnt euch und gebt Euch einen Kuß!   sich versöhnen

I'll **make** it **up** (to you) later.   to make(it)up –
Das mache ich später wieder gut.   wieder gutmachen

I can just about **manage**.   to manage – schaffen
Ich kann es kaum noch schaffen.

We'll **manage** one way or another.   to manage – schaffen
Wir schaffen es irgendwie.

MM MMM MM MMM MM MMM MM MMM MM MMM

I can't **manage** with three children!   to manage – schaffen
Ich kann es mit drei Kindern nicht schaffen!

It's bad **manners** to...   *– manners*
Es gehört sich nicht zu.......   sich gehören – to be proper

You're just **marking** time.   *– to mark*
Du vertreibst nur die Zeit.   vertreiben – to pass away

You'll make your **mark**!   *– mark*
Du wirst dich durchsetzen!   sich durchsetzen – to achieve

Study hard and get high **marks**.   marks – die Noten
Lern fleißig und bekomme gute Noten!

On your **marks**! Get set! Go!   *– marks*
Auf die Plätze! Fertig! Los!   die Plätze – the places

You're no **match** for him.   *– match*
Du kannst dich mit ihm nicht messen.   messen – to measure

No **matter** what I do...   *– matter*
Egal, was ich mache, ...   egal – all the same

That's quite another **matter**.   *– matter*
Das ist etwas ganz anderes.   etwas – something

As a **matter of fact**...   *– matter of fact*
Tatsächlich......   tatsächlich – as a matter of fact

What do you **mean** by that?   to mean – bedeuten
Was soll das bedeuten?

It would **mean** working hard.   to mean – bedeuten
Das würde viel Arbeit bedeuten.

MM MMM MM MMM MM MMM MM MMM MM MMM

You know very well what I **mean**!　　　　to mean – meinen
Du weißt ganz genau, was ich meine!

I **mean** it!　　　　　　　　　　　　　to mean – meinen
Ich meine es ernst!

You don't **mean** it!　　　　　　　　　　– *to mean*
Das kann nicht dein Ernst sein!　　　der Ernst – seriousness

It doesn't **mean** anything!　　　　　　　– *to mean*
Das hat keine Bedeutung!　　　　die Bedeutung – meaning

It **means** a lot to me!　　　　　　　　　– *to mean*
Mir liegt viel daran.　　　　　　　　liegen – to lie

That was a **mean** thing to say.　　　　mean – gemein
Was du gesagt hast, das war gemein!

That was a **mean** thing to do.　　　　mean – gemein
Was du getan hast, das war gemein.

If you get my **meaning**.　　　　　　　– *meaning*
Wenn du mich richtig verstehst.　　verstehen – to understand

There is more to this than **meets** the eye.　– *to meet*
Da steckt mehr dahinter, als man　　der Blick – glance
auf den ersten Blick sieht.

Sing it from **memory**!　　　　memory – das Gedächtnis
Sing es aus dem Gedächtnis!

I have a **memory** like a sieve.　　memory – das Gedächtnis
Ich habe ein schlechtes Gedächtnis.

106

MM MMM MM MMM MM MMM MM MMM MM MMM

You keep getting into/ a **mess**/ trouble/.   mess/ trouble – die
Du gerätst ständig in Schwierigkeiten!   Schwierigkeiten

Your bedroom's a **mess**!   mess – das Durcheinander
Dein Schlafzimmer ist ein Durcheinander!

Leave a **message** for me if you go out!   message – die Nachricht
Hinterlaß mir eine Nachricht, wenn du ausgehst!

You look **messy**!   messy – unordentlich
Du siehst unordentlich aus!

You **might** do that now.   might – könnte
Du könntest es jetzt machen

I've told you a **million** times!   – *million*
Das habe ich dir tausendmal gesagt!   tausend – thousand

I put it completely out of my **mind**!   mind – der Sinn
Ich habe es ganz aus dem Sinn geschlagen.

Is there something on your **mind**?   mind – der Sinn
Hast du etwas im Sinn?

What I **mind** is…   – *to mind*
Was mich stört, ist...   stören – to disturb

I've a good **mind** to play along.   – *mind*
Ich habe große Lust mitzuspielen.   die Lust – desire

Speak your **mind**.   – *mind*
Sag deine Meinung!   die Meinung – opinion

Many men, many minds.   minds – die Sinne
Viele Köpfe, viele Sinne.

MMM MM MMM MM MMM MM MMM MM MMM MM

Keep your **mind** on your work!   *– mind*
Bleib bei der Sache!   bl<u>ei</u>ben – to remain

I'm not a **mind reader**!   *– mind reader*
Ich bin kein Gedankenleser!   der Ged<u>a</u>nkenleser –
thought reader

Never **mind** about that now!   *– (never) mind*
Kümmere dich jetzt nicht d<u>a</u>rum!   sich k<u>ü</u>mmern – to worry
oneself

If we survive this, it will be a miracle!   miracle – das W<u>u</u>nder
Wenn wir d<u>ie</u>ses überst<u>e</u>hen, ist es ein W<u>u</u>nder!

You can't afford to **miss** school.   to miss – verp<u>a</u>ssen
Du kannst es dir nicht l<u>ei</u>sten, die Sch<u>u</u>le zu verp<u>a</u>ssen.

I **miss** you.   to miss – verm<u>i</u>ssen
Ich verm<u>i</u>sse dich.

Find the **missing/** word/ money/!   missing – f<u>e</u>hlend(e)
F<u>i</u>nde das f<u>e</u>hlende/ Wort/ Geld/!

You must have made a **mistake**.   mistake – der F<u>e</u>hler
Es kann sein, du hast <u>ei</u>nen F<u>e</u>hler gem<u>a</u>cht.

Unless I'm **mistaken**...   to be mistaken – sich t<u>äu</u>schen
Wenn ich mich nicht t<u>äu</u>sche....

There's been a **misunderstanding**.   misunderstanding – das
Es hat ein M<u>i</u>ßverständnis geg<u>e</u>ben.   Mißverständnis

I haven't a **moment** to spare!   moment – der M<u>o</u>ment
Ich h<u>a</u>be k<u>ei</u>nen M<u>o</u>ment frei!

MM MMM MM MMM MM MMM MM MMM MM MMM

Money doesn't grow on trees!   money – das Geld
Das Geld fällt nicht vom Himmel!

Just ask if you need **money**.   money – das Geld
Du brauchst bloß zu bitten, wenn du Geld brauchst.

I'm in no **mood** for jokes.   mood – die Laune
Ich bin nicht in der Laune, Witze zu hören.

Let's say no **more** about it.   more – mehr
Sagen wir nichts mehr davon!

It's just **more** of the same.   *– more*
Es ist immer nur das gleiche.   immer nur – just

Who(m) do you like **more**?   *– more*
Wen hast du lieber?   lieber – prefer

What **more** can I say?   *– more*
Was kann ich noch sagen?   noch – still

Some **mornings** you don't feel   mornings – morgens
like getting up!
Manchmal möchte man morgens gar nicht aufstehen!

You break the **mould**!   *– mould*
Du bist aus einem anderen Holzgeschnitzt!   das Holz – wood

Don't put words in my **mouth**!   mouth – der Mund
Dreh mir nicht das Wort im Mund herum!

Don't speak with your **mouth** full!   mouth – der Mund
Sprich nicht mit vollem Mund!

You've said a **mouthful**!   *– mouthful*
Du hast sehr viel gesagt!   sehr viel – very much

MM MMM MM MMM MM MMM MM MMM MM MMM

Could you **move**, please?   to move – bew<u>e</u>gen
K<u>ö</u>nntest du dich b<u>i</u>tte zur S<u>ei</u>te bewegen?

Why don't you make the first **move**?   move – der Zug
War<u>u</u>m machst du nicht den <u>e</u>rsten Zug?

Get a **move** on!   – *move*
Be<u>ei</u>l dich!   sich be<u>ei</u>len – to hurry

We have to **mow** the lawn.   to mow – m<u>ä</u>hen
Wir m<u>ü</u>ssen den R<u>a</u>sen m<u>ä</u>hen.

There isn't **much** we can do.   much – viel
Wir k<u>ö</u>nnen nicht sehr viel m<u>a</u>chen.

This is too **much**!   much – viel
Das ist zuv<u>ie</u>l!

That's a bit **much**!   – *much*
Das ist ein b<u>i</u>ßchen zuviel!   zuv<u>ie</u>l – too much

Take **as much** time as you like!   as much – sov<u>ie</u>l
Laß dir sov<u>ie</u>l Zeit wie du willst!

As much as I'd like to, I can't say yes.   – *as much as*
So g<u>e</u>rne wie ich m<u>ö</u>chte, kann ich nicht z<u>u</u>stimmen.   so – as

You seem to be in a **muddle**.   – *muddle*
Du scheinst v<u>ö</u>llig d<u>u</u>rcheinander   d<u>u</u>rcheinander – confused
zu sein.

We'll **muddle through**.   to muddle through – sich
Wir w<u>e</u>rden uns d<u>u</u>rchschlagen.   d<u>u</u>rchschlagen

It's **muggy**.   muggy – schwül
Es ist schwül.

110

You're getting away with **murder**!   – *murder*
Du kannst dir alles erlauben!   erlauben – allow

Leaving you with your sister is **murder**.   – *murder*
Dich mit deiner Schwester allein zu   unmöglich – impossible
lassen, ist unmöglich!

You **must** be hungry.   must, have to – müssen
Du mußt hungrig sein.,

We **must** do something   must, have to – müssen
about this problem.
Wir müssen etwas gegen dieses Problem unternehmen.

I did it all **myself**.   myself – selbst
Ich habe es selbst getan.

Be careful when you are climbing the tree.
Sei vorsichtig, wenn du auf den Baum steigst.
Zai FOHR-zikh-tikh, venn doo aouf dain baoum shtihkst.

Both of you can sit in the wagon.
Ihr beiden könnt im Wagen sitzen.
Ihr BIGH-d'n kehrnt im VAH-g'n ZIHT-ts'n.

Please don't pick the flowers!
Pfücke die Blumen bitte nicht!
FLEWK-keh dee BLUHM-e'n BIT-teh nihsht!

N

Do I have to **nag** you?
Muß ich das dir immer wieder sagen?

– to nag
sagen – to say, tell

Someone who shall remain **nameless**...
Jemand, der namenslos bleiben wird...

nameless – namenslos

Is someone calling you **names**?
Wirst du mit Schimpfwörtern
nachgerufen?

– names
die Schimpfwörter – curses

It's time to have a **nap.**
Es ist Zeit, ein Nickerchen zu machen.

nap – das Nickerchen

113

NN NNN NN NNN NN NNN NN NNN NN NNN NN NNN NN

That was a **nasty** fall.
Das war ein böser Sturz.

nasty – böse

It's only **natural** that you
would want to go.
Es ist nur selbstverständlich, daß du gehen möchtest.

natural – selbstverständlich

It's not in your **nature**.
Das entspricht nicht deiner Natur.

nature – die Natur

This is the **nearest** thing we have
to a playroom.
Dieses Zimmer kommt einem Spielzimmer am nächsten.

nearest – am nächsten

We don't have **nearly** enough time.
Wir haben bei weitem nicht genug Zeit.

nearly – bei weitem

We're **nearly** there. (Arrived)
Wir sind fast da.

nearly – fast

Your room looks so **neat**!
Dein Zimmer sieht ordentlich aus!

neat – ordentlich

Necessity is the mother of invention.
Not macht erfinderisch.

necessity – die Not

You're in this up to your **neck**!
Du steckst bis zum Hals drin!

neck – der Hals

You're sticking your **neck** out!
Du riskierst Kopf und Kragen.

– *neck*
der Kopf – head

That's all I **need**!
Das fehlt mir gerade noch!

– *to need*
fehlen – to be missing

NN NNN NN NNN NN NNN NN NNN NN NNN NN NNN NN

Need I say more?
Brauche ich mehr zu sagen?

to need – brauchen

It's like looking for a **needle** in a haystack.
Es ist, als ob man eine Stecknadel
im Heuhaufen suchte.

needle – die
    Stecknadel

Don't be so **negative**!
Sei nicht so negativ!

negative – negativ

Did you **neglect** to cut the lawn?
Hast du versäumt, den Rasen zu mähen?

to neglect – versäumen

That's **neither** here nor there.
Weder noch.

neither – weder

You've got a **nerve**!
Du hast Nerven!

nerve – der Nerv

I **never** expected this!
Ich habe so etwas nie erwartet!

never – nie

Well, I **never**!
So etwas!

– *never*
etwas – something

Never mind!
Macht nichts!

– *never*
machen – to make, do

That's nothing **new**!
Das ist nichts Neues!

new – Neu(es)

No news is good **news**.
Keine Nachricht ist auch eine Nachricht.

news – die Nachricht

115

NN NNN NN NNN NN NNN NN NNN NN NNN NN NNN NN

That's **news** to me! — *news*
Das ist mir ganz neu! neu – new

What shall we do **next**? next – nächstes
Was sollen wir als nächstes machen?

What did you do **next**? next – nächstes
Was hast du als nächstes gemacht?

It was **nice** of you to help. nice – nett
Es war nett von dir zu helfen.

That's a **nice** way to behave. nice – nett
Du hast dich sehr nett benommen.

Have a **nice** time! – *nice*
Hab viel Vergnügen! das Vergnügen – enjoyment

You got here in the **nick of time**! nick of time – der
Du bist im letzten Augenblick angekommen. Augenblick

We're going to **nip this in the bud**. to nip in the bud – im
Wir wollen es im Keim ersticken. Keim ersticken

Nod your head! to nod – nicken
Nick mit dem Kopf!

What's all that **noise**? noise – der Lärm
Was ist das für ein Lärm?

Don't make any **noise**! noise – der Lärm
Mach keinen Lärm!

It's so **noisy** in here! – *noisy*
Es ist hier sehr laut! laut – loud

We'll have **none** of that!
Jetzt reicht's aber!

– none
r**ei**chen – to be enough

Let's not have any **nonsense**.
Schluß mit dem **U**nsinn!

nonsense – der **U**nsinn

Look in all the **nooks and crannies**!
Schau in jeden W**i**nkel!

– nooks and crannies
der W**i**nkel – corner

You can't see beyond the end of
your **nose**.
Du bist sehr k**u**rzsichtig.

– nose
k**u**rzsichtig – short-sighted

I have **nothing** to do.
Ich h**a**be nichts zu tun.

nothing – nichts

It has **nothing** to do with you.
Es hat mit dir nichts zu tun.

nothing – nichts

You were **nowhere** to be found.
Man k**o**nnte dich n**i**rgendwo f**i**nden.

nowhere – n**i**rgendwo

This is a hard **nut** to crack. (Problem)
Das ist **ei**ne h**a**rte Nuß zu kn**a**cken.

nut – die Nuß

Swing, but don't swing too high!
Schaukle, aber schaukle nicht zu hoch!
SHAOU-kleh, AH-behr SHAOU-kleh nihsht tsoo hokh!

Go and hide!
Geh und versteck dich!
Gay unt fehr-STEKH dihsh!

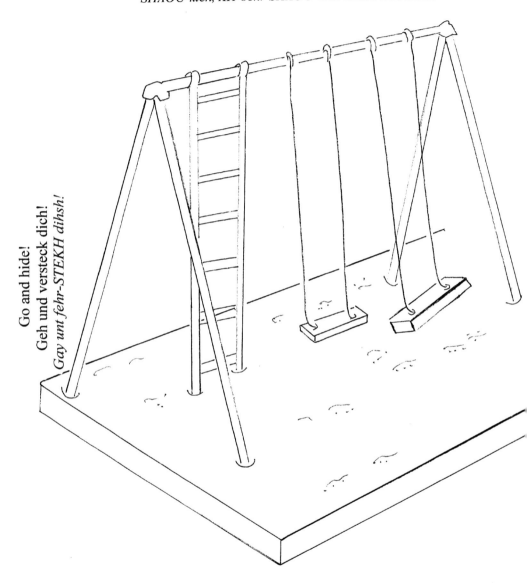

Slide down slowly!
Rutsch langsam hinunter!
Rutsh LANG-zahm hin-UHN-tehr!

O

I **object** to your doing that. Ich habe etwas dagegen, wenn du das machst.	*– to object* dagegen – against it
I see no **objection**. Ich habe nichts dagegen einzuwenden	*– objection* dagegen – against it
Much **obliged**. Ich bin dafür sehr dankbar.	*– obliged* dankbar – thankful
You were **oblivious** to what was going on. Du hast deine Umgebung gar nicht wahrgenommen!	*– oblivious* wahrnehmen – to perceive

OOO OO OOO OO OOO OO OOO OO OOO OO OOO OO

You're being **obstinate**.
Du bleibst stur.

obstinate – stur

When did that **occur** to you?
Wann ist es dir eingefallen?

to occur – einfallen

I'm **off**!
Ich gehe!

– *off*
gehen – to go

I don't know **offhand**.
Im Moment kann ich es dir nicht sagen.

– *offhand*
im Moment –
    at the moment

You're **old enough** to sleep by yourself.
Du bist alt genug, allein zu schlafen.

old enough – alt genug

What's **on** TV?
Was gibt es im Fernsehen?

on – im

One of us will be there to see you.
Einer von uns wird da sein, um dich zu sehen.

one of us – einer von uns

It's **only** me.
Ich bin's bloß.

only – bloß

You're not the **only one** here.
Du bist nicht der einzige, der hier ist.

only one – der/die/das
    einzige

Leave your **options** open!
Laß alle Möglichkeiten offen!

– *options*
die Möglichkeiten – possibilities

It won't **open**.
Es geht nicht auf.

open – auf

Did you do it **or** not?
Hast du oder hast du es nicht gemacht?

or – oder

120

OOO OO OOO OO OOO OO OOO OO OOO OO OOO

I don't take **orders** from you.
Ich lasse mir von dir nicht
herumkommandieren.

— *orders*
kommandieren — to
command, order

This is no **ordinary** picnic.
Es ist kein gewöhnliches Picknick.

ordinary — gewöhnlich

You **ought** not to worry so much!
Du sollst dir nicht soviel Sorgen machen!

ought — sollen

This **ought** to have been done before.
Man hätte es eher machen sollen.

ought — sollen

That's/ **out**/ unacceptable/.
Das geht nicht.

— *out*
gehen — to go

I'm **out** of ideas.
Ich habe keine Ideen mehr.

— *out*
kein — no, none

They're just **out** for a good time.
Sie wollen sich nur amüsieren.

— *out*
nur — only

You have to pay for it **out of**
your own money.
Das mußt du aus deinem eigenen Geld bezahlen.

out of — aus

You feel **out of it**.(not included)
Du fühlst dich wie ausgeschlossen.

out of it —ausgeschlossen

We're an **outdoor** family.
Wir sind eine naturliebende Familie.

— *outdoor*
naturliebende — nature-loving

You can sleep **outdoors** this weekend.
Du darfst dieses Wochenende im Freien schlafen.

outdoors — im Freien

OOO OO OOO OO OOO OO OOO OO OOO OO OOO OO

I'll meet you **outside** the library.   – *outside*
Ich treffe dich vor der Bibliothek.   vor – in front of

Can I read **over** your shoulder?   over – über
Darf ich dir über die Schulter schauen, wenn du liest?

Put a blanket **over** yourself!   over – über
Zieh eine Decke über dich!

I can't hear you **over** the noise.   – *over*
Ich kann dich bei dem Lärm nicht hören.   bei – with, at

Are you **over** your disappointment?   – *over*
Ist die Enttäuschung überstanden?   überstehen – to overcome

Over and over again.   over and over again –
Immer wieder.   immer wieder

Just get it **over with**!   – *over with*
Mach doch Schluß damit!   der Schluß – finish, conclusion

Don't **overdo** it. (work too hard)   to overdo – überanstrengen
Überanstrenge dich nicht!

Your library book is **overdue.**   overdue – überfällig
Dein Buch von der Bibliothek ist überfällig.

I'm **overjoyed**!   overjoyed – überglücklich
Ich bin überglücklich!

You're **overruled**!   overruled – überstimmt
Du bist überstimmt!

Don't **overstay** your welcome.   – *overstay*
Bleib nicht länger, als erwünscht ist.   länger – longer

OOO OO OOO OO OOO OO OOO OO OOO OO OOO OO

You're on your **own**!   own – <u>ei</u>genen
Du mußt auf <u>ei</u>genen F<u>ü</u>ßen st<u>e</u>hen!

It's my **own**.   own – <u>ei</u>genes
Das ist mein <u>ei</u>genes.

I have my **own** money.   own – <u>ei</u>genes
Ich h<u>a</u>be mein <u>ei</u>genes Geld.

You behave as if you **own** the place!   – *to own*
Du ben<u>i</u>mmst dich, als wenn dir der   geh<u>ö</u>ren – to belong to
Platz geh<u>ö</u>rt!

Own up!   to own up – z<u>u</u>geben
Gib zu!

I carry my baby in my pouch.
Ich trage mein Baby in meinem Beutel.
Ihsh TRAH-geh mighn BAY-beh ihn MIGH-n'm BOI-tehl.

I strut and crow.
Ich stolziere und krähe.
Ihsh SH'T'OHL-tseer-eh unt KREH-heh.

I have feathers.
Ich habe Federn.
Ihsh HAH-beh FEH-dehrn.

P

Pace yourself. Laß langsam gehen!	*– to pace* langsam – slow(ly)
Pack it in! (No complaining) Laß es gut sein!	*– to pack* gut – good
Don't be a **pain in the neck**! Geh mir nicht auf die Nerven!	*– a pain in the neck* die Nerven – nerves
Let's see how things **pan out**. Schauen wir, wie die Sachen auslaufen.	*– to pan out* auslaufen – to end

PP PPP PP PPP PP PPP PP PPP PP PPP PP PPP PP PPP PP

Don't get into a **panic**!   panic – die Panik
Gerate nicht in Panik!

Don't **panic**!   panic – die Panik
Nur keine Panik!

You've **parked** yourself in front   – *to park*
of the TV again!   pflanzen – to plant
Du hast dich schon wieder vor den Fernseher gepflanzt!

It's all **part** of growing up.   – *part*
Das gehört zum Erwachsenwerden.   gehören – to belong

I don't want any **part** of it!   – *part*
Ich will nicht daran beteiligt sein!   beteiligt – involved

Of course, I take your **part**.   – *part*
Sicher stehe ich dir zur Seite.   die Seite – side

I didn't notice anything in **particular**.   particular – besonderes
Ich habe nichts Besonderes gemerkt.

I'm not **particular**.   – *particular*
Es kommt mir nicht so darauf an.   darauf ankommen – to matter

You're awfully **particular** about the shirt. – *particular*
Du nimmst es mit dem Hemd sehr genau.   genau – exact(ly)

I'm **partway** through the book.   partway – zum Teil
Ich habe das Buch zum Teil gelesen.

You can't be a **party** to such a thing.   – *party*
Du kannst nicht daran beteiligt sein.   beteiligt – involved

PP PPP PP PPP PP PPP PP PPP PP PPP PP PPP PP PPP PP

The **party**'s over!
Jetzt ist's vorb<u>ei</u>!

– party
vorb<u>ei</u> – over

Let it **pass**!
Verg<u>e</u>ssen wir es!

– to pass
verg<u>e</u>ssen – to forget

I wouldn't put it **past** him.
Ich w<u>ü</u>rde es ihm schon z<u>u</u>trauen.

– past
z<u>u</u>trauen – to be capable of

I'm **past** caring.
Es k<u>ü</u>mmert mich nicht mehr.

– past
nicht mehr – no more

Patch things **up** with your sister!
Vers<u>ö</u>hne dich mit d<u>ei</u>ner Schw<u>e</u>ster!

– to patch up
sich vers<u>ö</u>hnen – to reconcile

I'm at the end of my **patience**.
Bei mir geht die Ged<u>u</u>ld zu <u>E</u>nde.

patience – die Ged<u>u</u>ld

You have tried my **patience** beyond measure.
Du hast m<u>ei</u>ne Ged<u>u</u>ld bis zum <u>E</u>nde getr<u>ie</u>ben.

patience – die Ged<u>u</u>ld

I've no **patience** with you.
Ich h<u>a</u>be k<u>ei</u>ne Ged<u>u</u>ld mit dir.

patience – die Ged<u>u</u>ld

I'm trying to be **patient** with you.
Ich vers<u>u</u>che mit dir ged<u>u</u>ldig zu sein.

patient – ged<u>u</u>ldig

I wouldn't do it if you **paid** me.
Ich w<u>ü</u>rde das nicht tun, auch wenn du mich bez<u>a</u>hlst.

to pay – bez<u>a</u>hlen

Pay attention.
Paß auf!

– to pay
<u>au</u>fpassen – to pay attention

Give grandma a **peck** on the cheek!
Gib <u>O</u>ma ein K<u>ü</u>ßchen auf die W<u>a</u>nge!

peck (kiss) – das K<u>ü</u>ßchen

127

PP PPP PP PPP PP PPP PP PPP PP PPP PP PPP PP PPP PP

How **peculiar**!   pecular – komisch
Wie komisch!

Have a **peek**!   – to peek
Schau mal kurz hin!   hinschauen – to look at

Keep your eyes **peeled** for the bus!   – peeled
Paß auf, bis der Bus kommt!   aufpassen – to pay attention

I don't want to hear another **peep**   peep – der Pieps
out of you!
Ich will von dir keinen Pieps hören!

A **penny** for your thoughts.   – penny
Ich möchte deine Gedanken lesen können.   lesen – to read

I don't expect you to be **perfect**.   perfect – perfekt
Ich erwarte nicht, daß du perfekt bist.

Perish the thought!   – to perish
Gott bewahre!   bewahren – to keep, save

Perk up!   – to perk up
Sei aufmerksam!   aufmerksam – alert

You have to ask **permission** to do that. permission – die
Du mußt um Erlaubnis bitten, das zu tun.   Erlaubnis

It might be better to ask **permission** first. permission – die
Es wäre besser, zuerst um Erlaubnis zu   Erlaubnis
bitten.

You're not **permitted** to do that.   to (be) permitted – dürfen
Das darfst du nicht machen.

128

PP PPP PP PPP PP PPP PP PPP PP PPP PP PPP PP PPP PP PPP PP

You're **perpetual** motion!
Du bist ewig in Bewegung!

perpetual – ewig

Don't take it **personally**!
Nimm es nicht persönlich!

personal – persönlich

Who's on the **phone**?
Wer ist am Telefon?

phone – das Telefon

I have a bone to **pick** with you!
Ich habe mit dir ein Hühnchen zu rupfen.

– to pick
to pluck – rupfen

This will **pick** you **up**.
Dies wird dich aufheitern.

to pick up – aufheitern

Let's **pick up** where we left off.
Machen wir da weiter, wo wir aufgehört haben.

– to pick up
weitermachen – to continue

I'll only have a small **piece** (of cake).
Ich möchte nur ein kleines Stück Kuchen.

piece – das Stück

I'm glad to see you're still in one **piece**.
Es freut mich, daß du unverletzt davon gekommen bist.

–piece
unverletzt – uninjured

It's a **piece of cake**! (easy)
Das ist ein Kinderspiel!

– piece of cake
das Kinderspiel – child's play

I'd like to give you a **piece of my mind**!
Ich möchte dir meine Meinung sagen!

– piece of my mind
die Meinung – opinion

Don't go all to **pieces**!
Dreh nicht durch!

– pieces
durchdrehen – to go to pieces

129

PP PPP PP PPP PP PPP PP PPP PP PPP PP PPP PP PPP PP

You're making a **pig** of yourself!   *– pig*
Du überißt dich wieder!   überessen – to overeat

If **pigs** could fly!   *– pig*
Fantasie, verlaß mich nicht!   die Fantasie – fantasy

Piggyback – that's fun!   piggyback – huckepack
Huckepack – das macht Spaß!

I've got a **pile** of things to do!   pile – der Haufen
Ich habe einen Haufen Aufträge zu erledigen!

Don't **pin** the blame on your brother.   *– to pin*
Beschuldige nicht deinen Bruder.   beschuldigen – to blame

It's the **pits**!   *– pits*
So ein Mist!   der Mist – manure

This is no **place** for you.   place – der Platz
Hier ist kein Platz für dich.

You have to be in the right **place** at   place – die Stelle
the right time.
Man muß an der richtigen Stelle zur richtigen Zeit sein.

Put yourself in my **place**.   place – die Stelle
Tu, als wenn du an meiner Stelle wärest

I can't be in two **places** at once!   place – die Stelle
Ich kann nicht zur gleichen Zeit an zwei Stellen sein.

You'll go **places**!   *– places*
Du bringst es zu etwas!   etwas – something

It's as **plain** as the nose on your face!   *– plain*
Das sieht doch ein Blinder!   der Blinde – the blind person

PP PPP PP PPP PP PPP PP PPP PP PPP PP PPP PP PPP PP

I'll be quite **plain** with you. — *plain*
Ich werde es dir ganz klarmachen. klarmachen – to make clear

Plan ahead! to plan – planen
Plane voraus!

Do you have other **plans**? plans – die Pläne
Hast du andere Pläne?

There's been a change of **plans**. plans – die Pläne
Man hat die Pläne geändert.

Play fair. to play – spielen
Spiel fair!

Have you anything to **play** with? to play – spielen
Hast du etwas, mit dem du spielen kannst?

You do as you **please** to please – gefallen
Du machst es, wie es dir gefällt.

Please yourself! to please – gefallen
Tu, was dir gefällt!

There's no **pleasing** you. to please – recht machen
Man kann es dir nicht recht machen.

There's no **pleasing** everybody. to please – recht machen
Man kann es nicht allen recht machen.

Please God! — *please*
Lieber Gott! lieber – dear

I am **pleased** with you. pleased – zufrieden
Ich bin mit dir zufrieden

I was not altogether **pleased**.
Ich war nicht total damit zufrieden.

pleased – zufrieden

What are you/ **plotting**/ up to?
Was hast du vor?

– *to plot*
vorhaben – to plan

Here is some **pocket** money.
Hier ist etwas Taschengeld.

pocket – die Tasche

Don't **point** at that man!
Zeig nicht mit dem Finger auf den Mann!

to point – zeigen

That's not the **point**.
Darum geht es nicht.

– *point*
darum – about that

What's the **point**?
Worum geht es?

– *point*
worum – about what

I don't see the **point**.
Ich verstehe nicht, worum es geht.

– *point*
worum – about what

That's beside the **point**.
Das spielt keine Rolle.

– *point*
die Rolle – role

Get to the **point**!
Komm zur Sache!

– *point*
die Sache – thing

I'm not **poking fun** at you.
Ich mache mich nicht lustig über dich

– *to poke fun*
sich lustig machen –
    to make fun of

Poor thing!
Armes Ding!

poor thing
das Ding – thing

PP PPP PP PPP PP PPP PP PPP PP PPP PP PPP PP PPP PP

You won't make yourself very
popular doing that.
Du machst dich nicht sehr beliebt, wenn du das tust.

popular – beliebt

You're in no **position** to ask now.
Du bist nicht in der Lage, jetzt zu fragen.

position – die Lage

What **possessed** you to do that!
Was ist bloß in dich gefahren, das zu tun.

– *possessed*
fahren – to travel

If at all **possible**...
Wenn es überhaupt möglich ist....

possible – möglich

Anything is **possible**.
Alles ist möglich.

possible – möglich

Our **prayers** have been answered.
Der liebe Gott hat unsere Gebete gehört.

prayer – das Gebet

Say your **prayers**.
Bete.

– *prayer*
beten – to pray

Why are you **pretending** you're sick?
Warum täuschst du eine Krankheit vor?

to pretend – vortäuschen

Not at any **price**!
Um keinen Preis!

price – der Preis

You're our **pride** and joy.
Du bist unser ganzer Stolz!

pride – der Stolz

You're in the **prime** of life!
Du bist in der Blüte deiner Jahre!

– *prime*
die Blüte – the bloom

How shall we **proceed**?
Wie sollen wir weitermachen?

to proceed –
weitermachen

133

PP PPP PP PPP PP PPP PP PPP PP PPP PP PPP PP PPP PP

Promise me to behave. to promise – versprechen
Versprich mir, du benimmst dich (gut).

You **promised** me you'd do it. to promise – versprechen
Du hast mir versprochen, du tust es.

We're **proud** of you. proud – stolz
Wir sind stolz auf dich.

You've done us **proud**. proud – stolz
Du hast uns stolz gemacht.

Talking to you is like **pulling** teeth! to pull – ziehen
Man muß dir jedes Wort aus dem Mund ziehen!

Don't **push** yourself too hard! to push – anstrengen
Streng dich nicht zuviel an!

Don't **push** her out of the way! to push – schieben
Schieb sie nicht aus dem Weg!

I'm a **pushover**. – *pushover*
Ich bin ein leichtes Opfer. das Opfer – victim

Put some paper under it! to put – legen
Leg etwas Papier darunter!

Put your back into it! to put – stecken
Steck Mühe in deine Arbeit!

Put it anywhere! to put – stellen
Stell es irgendwohin!

Put yourself in my position! to put – sich versetzen
Versetz dich in meine Situation!

Put it there! (Handshake, Hi five!)   *– to put*
Gib mal die Hand!   g<u>e</u>ben – to give

I'm **putting** my foot down.   *– to put*
Jetzt ist Schluß!   der Schluß – conclusion

You can really **put** it **away**!   *– to put away*
Du kannst dich w<u>i</u>rklich v<u>o</u>llstopfen!   v<u>o</u>llstopfen – to stuff

Put the game **back** where it belongs.   to put back – zur<u>ü</u>cklegen
Leg das Spiel w<u>ie</u>der zur<u>ü</u>ck, wo es h<u>i</u>ngehört!

You can't **put down** that book!   to put down – l<u>e</u>gen
Du kannst das Buch <u>ei</u>nfach nicht aus der Hand l<u>e</u>gen!

Stop **putting** it **off**!   to put off – versch<u>ie</u>ben
Versch<u>ie</u>b es nicht <u>i</u>mmer auf sp<u>ä</u>ter!

I like where you **put up** that poster.   to put up – <u>au</u>fhängen
Es gef<u>ä</u>llt mir, wo du das P<u>o</u>ster <u>au</u>fgehängt hast.

I want a campsite right on the lake.
Ich will einnen Campingplatz direkt am See.
Ihsh vill IGH-n'n KAHM-ping-plahts dee-REKT ahm zeh.

Let's pitch the tent.
Lass uns das Zelt aufschlagen.
Lahs oons dahs tselt AOUF-shlah-g'n.

Set up the stove.
Stell den Kocher auf!
Shtell dain KOSH-ehr aouf!

Q

Let's not **quarrel** about this.
Wir wollen uns nicht darüber streiten.

to quarrel – streiten

I'm not picking a **quarrel** with you.
Ich fange mit dir keinen Streit an.

quarrel – der Streit

It's only a **question** of time.
Es ist nur eine Frage der Zeit.

question – die Frage

In answer to your **question**…
In Beantwortung deiner Frage ....

question – die Frage

QQ QQQ QQ QQQ QQ QQQ QQ QQQ QQ QQQ QQ QQQ

That's out of the **question**!   question – die Frage
Das kommt gar nicht in Frage!

That was **quick**!   quick – schnell
Das war schnell!

You have a **quick** temper.   *– quick*
Du kannst sehr jähzornig werden.   jähzornig – quick-tempered

Could you be **quiet**, please!   quiet – ruhig
Bitte, sei ruhig!

Let's call it **quits**.   to quit – aufhören
Hören wir damit auf!

R

I'll **race** you home!
Ich mache mit dir ein Wettrennen
nach Hause!

       – *to race*
das Wettrennen – race

I've been **racking** my brain!
Ich zerbreche mir den Kopf!

       – *to rack*
zerbrechen – to break

It never **rains** but it pours.
Ein Unglück kommt selten allein.

       – *to rain*
das Unglück – misfortune

You're as right as **rain**.
Du hast hundertprozentig recht.

       – *rain*
recht – right

RR RRR RR RRR RR RRR RR RRR RR RRR RR RRR RR

You're **rambling** on.
Du redest ununterbrochen Unsinn!

– to ramble
reden – to talk

Stop **ranting and raving**!
Hör auf so herumzuschimpfen!

– to rant and rave
herumschimpfen – to yell
and scream

I smell a **rat**!
Da ist etwas faul!

– rat
faul – rotten

At this **rate** we'll be here forever!
Bei diesem Tempo bleiben wir ewig hier!

rate – das Tempo

/**Rather**/ Better/ you than me!
Lieber du als ich!

rather – lieber

I thought it was **rather** good.
Ich habe es ziemlich gut gefunden.

rather – ziemlich

Can you **read** my mind?
Kannst du meine Gedanken lesen?

to read – lesen

I can't **read** the future.
Ich kann nicht in die Zukunft
schauen.

– to read
schauen – to look

You aren't anywhere near **ready** yet.
Du bist längst nicht soweit.

ready – soweit

What's the **real** reason?
Was ist der wirkliche Grund?

real – wirklich

It's **really** good.
Das ist echt gut.

really – echt

RR RRR RR RRR RR RRR RR RRR RR RRR RR RRR RR

That's no **reason** for giving up!   reason – der Grund
Es ist kein Grund aufzugeben!

Give me one good **reason**   reason – der Grund
why I should (do it).
Gib mir einen guten Grund, warum ich (es machen) soll.

Let's be **reasonable**!   reasonable – vernünftig
Seien wir vernünftig!

Be **reasonable**!   reasonable – vernünftig
Sei vernünftig!

The **day of reckoning** has arrived.   *– (day of) reckoning*
Der Tag der Abrechnung ist   die Abrechnung – settlement
gekommen.

For the **record**…   *– record*
Der Ordnung halber....   die Ordnung – order

You're as **red** as a beet!   red – rot
Du bist so rot wie eine Tomate!

You've turned all **red**.   red – rot
Du bist ganz rot geworden.

We have a good **relationship**.   relationship – das Verhältnis
Wir haben ein gutes Verhältnis.

I don't **relish** the idea.   to relish – schwärmen
Ich schwärme nicht für die Idee.

I'm **relying** on you to do it!   to rely on – sich verlassen auf
Ich verlasse mich darauf, daß du es tust.

RR RRR RR RRR RR RRR RR RRR RR RRR RR RRR RR

That **remains** to be seen. — *to remain*
Das müssen wir erst mal sehen. sehen – to see

The difficult part is **remembering**. to remember – sich erinnern
Es ist schwierig, sich daran zu erinnern.

As far back as I can **remember**. to remember – sich erinnern
So weit ich mich erinnern kann.

You don't need to **remind** me. to remind – erinnern
Du brauchst mich nicht daran zu erinnern.

School **reopens** in September. — *to reopen*
Das Schuljahr beginnt im wiederbeginnen – to begin
September wieder. again

I won't **repeat** this (more than once). to repeat – wiederholen
Ich werde es nicht (mehr als einmal) wiederholen.

I **resent** that! to resent – sich verbieten
Ich verbiete mir das.

You're **resentful**, I know. resentful – abstoßend
Ich weiß, du bist sehr abstoßend.

I **reserve** judgement. to reserve – zurückhalten
Ich halte mit einem Urteil zurück.

You're **resilient**. resilient – unverwüstlich
Du bist unverwüstlich.

I couldn't **resist** telling you. to resist – widerstehen
Ich konnte es nicht widerstehen, es dir zu erzählen.

142

RR RRR RR RRR RR RRR RR RRR RR RRR RR RRR RR

I can't **resist** chocolates!   to resist – widerstehen
Ich kann Schokolade nicht widerstehen!

You always take the line of   resistance – der Widerstand
  least **resistance.**
Du nimmst immer den Weg, wo der wenigste Widerstand ist.

You should **respect** your elders.   respect – der Respekt
Du sollst vor den Älteren Respekt haben.

I'm holding you **responsible.**   responsible – verantwortlich
Ich halte dich verantwortlich.

I **rest** my case!   to rest – ruhen
Ich lasse den Fall ruhen!

Give it a **rest!**   to rest – ruhen
Laß es ruhen!

Put your mind to **rest.**   – to rest
Beruhige dich!   sich beruhigen – to calm oneself

The **rest of us** want to go too.   rest of us – der Rest von uns
Der Rest von uns will auch gehen.

I had a **restless** night.   restless – unruhig
Ich hatte eine unruhige Nacht.

I have to **rethink** that.   to rethink – sich überlegen
Das muß ich mir noch einmal überlegen.

Revenge is sweet.   revenge – die Rache
Die Rache ist süß.

Quite the/ opposite/ **reverse/.**   reverse – umgekehrt
Total umgekehrt.

RR RRR RR RRR RR RRR RR RRR RR RRR RR RRR RR

Can you **ride** a bicycle?   to ride – f<u>a</u>hren
Kannst du F<u>a</u>hrrad f<u>a</u>hren?

That's just plain **ridiculous**.   ridiculous – l<u>ä</u>cherlich
Das ist <u>ei</u>nfach l<u>ä</u>cherlich.

You should know **right**   right – das Recht
from wrong.
Du sollst Recht und <u>U</u>nrecht <u>au</u>seinanderhalten k<u>ö</u>nnen.

You don't have the **right**   right – das Recht
to do that.
Du hast kein Recht, das zu tun.

It will all come **right** for you.   right – das R<u>e</u>chte
Es wird sich für dich zum R<u>e</u>chten k<u>o</u>mmen.

You will find that I am **right**.   right – recht
Du wirst f<u>e</u>ststellen, daß ich recht h<u>a</u>be.

You're half **right**.   right – recht
Du hast nur zur Hälfte recht.

It was the **right** thing to do.   right – r<u>i</u>chtig
Es war das R<u>i</u>chtige, was du getan hast.

I'll be **right** with you.   right – sof<u>o</u>rt
Ich k<u>o</u>mme sof<u>o</u>rt zu dir.

Let's put things **right**!   *– right*
Br<u>i</u>ngen wir <u>a</u>lles w<u>ie</u>der in <u>O</u>rdnung!   die <u>O</u>rdnung – order

Stay **right** behind me!   *– right*
Bleib dir<u>e</u>kt h<u>i</u>nter mir!   dir<u>e</u>kt – directly

144

RR RRR RR RRR RR RRR RR RRR RR RRR RR RRR RR

You seem to be **right-handed**.
Du scheinst, rechtshändig zu sein.

right-handed – rechtshändig

You did the **right thing**.
Du hast das Richtige gemacht.

right thing – das Richtige

That **rings** true.
Das klingt richtig.

– *to ring*
klingen – to sound

Rinse your hands!
Wasch dir die Hände!

to rinse – waschen

I'll read you the **riot act**!
Ich werde dir den Marsch blasen!

– *riot act*
der Marsch – march

What a **rip-off**!
So ein Betrug!

rip-off – der Betrug

Rise and shine!
Steh auf und sei munter!

– *to rise and shine*
aufstehen – to get up

He certainly gets a **rise out of** you!
Er kann dich immer reizen!

– *rise out of*
reizen – to provoke

That's a/ **risk**/ chance/ we'll
have to take!
Auf dieses Risiko gehen wir ein!

risk – das Risiko

I'm taking no/ **risks**/ chances/.
Ich gehe auf kein Risiko ein.

risk – das Risiko

At the risk of sounding foolish…
Auf die Gefahr hin, dumm
zu erscheinen.....

– *risk*
die Gefahr – danger

145

RR RRR RR RRR RR RRR RR RRR RR RRR RR RRR RR

A few years down the **road**   *– road*
and you'll change your mind.   das Jahr – year
In ein paar Jahren wirst du deine Meinung ändern.

Let's get this show on the **road**!   *– road*
Los geht's, Leut'!   los – start

I heard you **roar** with laughter!   to roar – brüllen
Ich habe gehört, wie du vor Lachen gebrüllt hast.

Don't **roll** your eyes!   to roll – rollen
Laß nicht die Augen rollen!

Start the ball **rolling**!   to roll – rollen
Bring den Stein ins Rollen!

Roll up your sleeves and get   to roll up – hochkrempeln
to work!
Kremple die Ärmel hoch und mach dich an die Arbeit!

I'm not **rolling in** money!   *– to roll in*
Ich schwimme nicht im Geld!   schwimmen – to swim

Don't **hit the roof**!   *– (to hit the) roof*
Spring nicht an die Decke!   an die Decke springen – to jump
                                         to the ceiling

Is there **room** for one more?   room – der Platz
Ist da Platz für noch einen?

There's no **room**.   room – der Platz
Es ist kein Platz.

Make **room** for your brother!   room – der Platz
Mach Platz für deinen Bruder!

146

RR RRR RR RRR RR RRR RR RRR RR RRR RR RRR RR

Money is the **root** of all evil.
Geld ist die Wurzel aller Übel.

root – die Wurzel

You're playing **rough**.
Du spielst rauh.

rough – rauh

Don't give me that **routine**!
Sag mir bloß nicht das Gleiche!

– routine
das Gleiche – the same (thing)

That's a load of **rubbish**!
Das ist reiner Quatsch!

rubbish – der Quatsch

Don't be **rude** to me!
Sei nicht unhöflich zu mir!

rude – unhöflich

You're getting a **rude** awakening.
Du wirst ein böses Erwachen
erleben.

– rude
böse(s) – nasty

There's no call for **rudeness**!
Das ist kein Grund, unhöflich zu sein!

– rudeness
unhöflich – rude

You're going to **ruin** your eyes.
Du verdirbst dir die Augen.

to ruin – verderben

Dinner's **ruined**!
Das Abendessen ist ruiniert!

ruined – ruiniert

It's against the **rules**.
Es ist gegen die Regeln.

rule – die Regel

The **rule** is you must make your bed.
Die Regel ist , du sollst dein Bett machen.

rule – die Regel

There's a **rumor** going around that…	rumor – das Gerücht
Es geht ein Gerücht herum. daß....	
Run like mad!	to run – laufen
Lauf wie verrückt!	
I'm just **running** to the store.	to run – laufen
Ich laufe nur zum Geschäft.	
I'll **run** you to school.	– *to run*
Ich bringe dich zur Schule.	bringen – to bring
Who's **running** this show?	– *to run*
Wer leitet das Geschehen?	leiten – to lead
You're **running** late.	– *to run*
Du hast Verspätung	die Verspätung – delay

S

Play it **safe**!	safe – sicher
Geh auf Nummer Sicher!	

You're in **safe** hands.	safe – sicher(en)
Du bist in sicheren Händen.	

Better **safe** than sorry.	*– safe*
Vorsicht ist besser als Nachsicht.	die Vorsicht – caution

Safe and sound.	*– safe and sound*
Gesund und wohlbehalten	gesund – healthy

SS SSS SS SSS SS SSS SS SSS SS SSS SS SSS SS SSS SS SSS

I have never **said** such a thing!
Ich habe so etwas nie gesagt.

said – gesagt

There's a lot to be **said** for that.
Das könnte vom Vorteil sein.

– *said*
der Vorteil – advantage

For heaven's **sake**!
Um Gottes willen.

sake – willen

The house isn't the **same** without you.
Das Haus ist nicht dasselbe ohne dich.

same – dasselbe

It's all the **same** to me. (I'm not fussy.)
Es ist mir alles egal!

same – egal

If it's all the **same** to you...
Wenn es dir ganz gleich ist...

same – gleich

It all amounts to the **same thing**.
Alles kommt aufs gleiche hinaus.

same thing – das gleiche

Your dad would tell you the **same thing**.
Dein Vater würde dir das gleiche sagen.

same thing – das gleiche

I don't care what/ he/ she/ **says**.
Es ist mir egal, was er/sie sagt.

to say – sagen

What did I say?
Was habe ich gesagt?

to say – sagen

Don't pay attention to what/ he/ she/ **says**.
Achte nicht auf das, was/ er/ sie/ sagt.

to say – sagen

You were right not to **say** anything.
Du hast recht gehabt, nichts zu sagen.

to say – sagen

150

SS SSS SS SSS SS SSS SS SSS SS SSS SS SSS SS SSS SS SSS SS SSS

What do you have to **say** for yourself.   to say – sagen
Was kannst du zu deiner Verteidung sagen?

You can **say** that again!   to say – sagen
Das kann man wohl sagen!

Need I **say** more?   to say – sagen
Brauche ich mehr zu sagen?

You have no **say** in the matter.   to say – sagen
Bei dieser Sache hast du nichts zu sagen.

You don't **say**!   – *to say*
Oh, wirklich!   wirklich – really

As I was **saying**…   – *saying*
Wie ich schon gesagt habe...   gesagt – said

You gave me an awful/ **scare**/ fright/.   scare – der Schreck
Du hast mir einen furchtbaren Schreck eingejagt.

You look **scared** to death!   scared – verängstigt
Du siehst verängstigt aus.

You have **scattered** crumbs all   scattered – verstreut
over the place!
Du hast überall Krümel verstreut.

Don't make a **scene**!   scene – die Szene
Mach doch keine Szene!

We all need a change of **scenery**!   – *scenery*
Wir alle brauchen eine schöne   die Abwechslung – change
Abwechslung!

SS SSS SS SSS SS SSS SS SSS SS SSS SS SSS SS SSS SS SSS

Everything went according to **schedule**.   – *schedule*
Es ist alles nach Plan verlaufen.   der Plan – plan

No **school** tomorrow!   – *school*
Morgen ist schulfrei!   schulfrei – school free

What's the **score**?   – *score*
Wie steht's?   stehen – to stand

It's just a **scratch**.   scratch – der Kratzer
Es ist bloß ein Kratzer.

I'm having **second** thoughts about that.   – *second*
Ich habe Bedenken dabei.   das Bedenken – reservations,
                                   misgivings

I'll let you in on a **secret**.   secret – das Geheimnis
Ich erzähle dir ein Geheimnis.

This is how I **see** it.   to see – sehen
So sehe ich die Sache.

Let me **see**./ Let's **see**.   to see – sehen
Laß mal sehen!

I'll **see** what I can do.   to see – sehen
Ich sehe, was ich machen kann.

We'll soon **see** about that!   to see – sehen
Das wollen wir erst mal sehen!

Don't let me **see** you here again.   to see – sehen
Ich will dich nicht wieder hier sehen.

Now **see** what you've done!   to see – sehen
Sieh nun mal, was du getan hast!

SS SSS SS SSS SS SSS SS SSS SS SSS SS SSS SS SSS SS SSS SS SSS

See for yourself!
Sieh das dir selber an!

to see – sehen

We shall see.
Warten wir mal ab!

– to see
abwarten – to wait for

Go and see!
Sieh doch mal nach!

– to see
nachsehen – to check

See to it that…
Bitte, sorg dafür, daß...

– to see
sorgen – to see to

I see what you mean.
Ich verstehe, was du meinst.

– to see
verstehen – to understand

It remains to be seen.
Das wird sich zeigen.

– to see
zeigen – to show

Seeing is believing.
Was man sieht, das glaubt man.

– seeing
sehen – to see

It doesn't seem right.
Das scheint mir nicht richtig zu sein.

to seem – scheinen

You seem tired.
Du siehst müde aus.

– to seem
aussehen – to look

You can't seem to get it right.
Es sieht aus, als wenn du es nicht richtig
machen kannst.

– to seem
aussehen – to look

They're selling like hot cakes!
Sie verkaufen sich wie warme Semmeln!

to sell – verkaufen

I'll send out for pizza.
Ich lasse Pizza liefern.

– to send out for
liefern – to deliver

SS SSS SS SSS SS SSS SS SSS SS SSS SS SSS SS SSS SS SSS SS SSS

You have a wonderful **sense** of direction.   sense – der Sinn
Du hast einen sehr guten Orientierungsinn.

There's no **sense** in worrying.   sense – der Sinn
Es hat keinen Sinn, sich Sorgen zu machen.

That makes (no) **sense**.   sense – der Sinn
Das macht (k)einen Sinn.

It makes little **sense**.   sense – der Sinn
Das macht wenig Sinn.

I've lost all **sense** of time.   – *sense*
Ich habe das Gefühl für die Zeit verloren. das Gefühl – the feeling

I like your **sense** of humor.   – *sense*
Deinen Humor finde ich gut.   der Humor – (sense of) humor

It makes perfect **sense**.   – *sense*
Das ist sehr vernünftig.   vernünftig – sensible

I **sense** that you are unhappy.   – *to sense*
Ich fühle, du bist unglücklich.   fühlen – to feel

That's the **sensible** thing to do.   sensible – vernünftig
Es ist sehr vernünftig, das zu tun.

You're overly **sensitive**.   sensitive – empfindlich
Du bist sehr empfindlich.

You can't be **serious**!   – *serious*
Das kann nicht dein Ernst sein!   der Ernst – seriousness

You take yourself too **seriously**.   seriously – ernst
Du nimmst dich zu ernst.

SS SSS SS SSS SS SSS SS SSS SS SSS SS SSS SS SSS SS SSS SS SSS

If my memory **serves** me correctly... *– to serve*
Wenn mein Gedächtnis mich nicht im Stich – in the lurch
im Stich läßt....

It **serves** you right! *– to serve*
Das geschieht dir ganz recht. geschehen – to happen

Are you all **set**? *– set*
Alles klar? klar – clear

I'm dead **set against** your going. *– (to be) set against*
Ich bin total dagegen, daß du gehst. dagegen – against it

Set aside enough time to go to the dentist. *– to set aside*
Nimm dir genügend Zeit, um zum Zahnarzt nehmen – to take
zu gehen.

You've been **set up**! *– (to be) set up*
Das will dir einer anhängen anhängen – to blame for

Take this to **settle** your stomach. *– to settle*
Nimm dieses ein, um deinen Magen beruhigen – to calm
zu beruhigen.

That **settles** it! to settle – erledigen
Damit wäre der Fall erledigt!

You look **shabby**. shabby – schäbig
Du siehst schäbig aus.

Don't **shake** your head! (no) to shake – schütteln
Schüttle nicht mit dem Kopf!

You're **shaking** like a leaf. to shake – zittern
Du zitterst wie Espenlaub.

SS SSS SS SSS SS SSS SS SSS SS SSS SS SSS SS SSS SS SSS

Shake hands.   *– to shake*
Gebt euch die Hände.   geben – to give

This place is a **shambles**!   shambles – das Durcheinander
Hier herrscht ein heilloses Durcheinander!

Shame on you!   to shame – schämen
Schäm dich!

What a **shame**!   *– shame*
Wie schade.   schade – too bad

You're out of **shape**!   shape – die Form
Du bist nicht in Form.

You don't do your **share**.   share – der Teil
Du erfüllst nicht deinen Teil.

Share and **share** alike!   to share – beteiligen
Beteiligt euch gleich daran!

That was a close **shave**!   *– shave*
Das war knapp!   knapp – very close

It's **sheer** madness!   sheer – rein(er)
Das ist reiner Wahnsinn!

What a **shock**!   shock – der Schock
So ein Schock!

Cut the visit **short**!   *– short*
Bleib nicht so lang!   lang – long

We're running **short** of milk.   *– short*
Wir haben nicht mehr viel Milch.   viel – a lot

156

SS SSS SS SSS SS SSS SS SSS SS SSS SS SSS SS SSS SS SSS SS

You're gone like a **shot**!
Du bist fort wie der Blitz!

– shot
der Blitz – lightning

You're a good **shot**!
Du bist ein guter Schütze!

– shot
der Schütze – marksman

You don't call the **shots**!
Du hast nicht das Sagen!

– shots
das Sagen – say

You of all people **should** know that.
Du von allen sollst das wissen.

should – sollen

You **should** do it right away.
Du sollst es sofort machen.

should – sollen

You **should**n't laugh at him.
Du sollst ihn nicht auslachen.

should – sollen

You **should** have seen the expression
on your face!
Du hättest deinen Gesichtsausdruck sehen sollen.

should – sollen

Don't shrug your **shoulders**!
Zuck nicht mit den Schultern!

shoulders – die Schultern

I would appreciate it if you didn't **shout**!
Ich wäre dankbar, wenn du nicht schreist!

to shout – schreien

Stop **shouting**!
Hör auf zu schreien!

to shout – schreien

Show them what you're made of!
Zeig ihnen, was in dir steckt!

to show – zeigen

Good **show**! Well done!
Bravo! Gut gemacht!

– show
Bravo – cheers

157

SS SSS SS SSS SS SSS SS SSS SS SSS SS SSS SS SSS SS SSS SS SSS SS

I **shudder** to think of it.   *– to shudder*
Mir graut, wenn ich daran denke.   grauen – to dread

I feel like a **shuttle service**.   shuttle service – der Pendeldienst
Ich komme mir vor wie ein Pendeldienst.

Don't **shy away** from doing that.   to shy away – scheuen
Scheu dich nicht davor!

You're going to make yourself **sick**.   sick – krank
Du wirst dich krank machen.

Come in the **side** door!   side – die Seite
Komm durch die Seitentür herein!

Look on the bright **side**!   side – die Seite
Betrachte es von der positiven Seite!

I am on your **side**.   side – die Seite
Ich bin auf deiner Seite.

You won't get on the right **side**   *– (right) side*
of me like that!   der Fuß – foot
So stellst du dich mit mir nicht auf guten Fuß!

Don't get on the wrong **side** of him.   *– side*
Du willst mit ihm nicht auf schlechtem   der Fuß – foot
Fuß stehen.

I'm not taking **sides**.   *– to side with*
Ich bleibe unparteiisch.   unparteiisch – impartial

You're a **sight** for sore eyes.   sight – der Anblick
Du bist ein freudiger Anblick.

SS SSS SS SSS SS SSS SS SSS SS SSS SS SSS SS SSS SS SSS

Out of **sight**, out of mind.
Aus den A̱ugen, aus dem Sinn.

– sight
die A̱ugen – eyes

You look a **sight**! (messy)
Du siehst ṵnmöglich aus!

– sight
au̱ssehen – to look

You have set your **sights** too high.
Du hast de̱ine Zi̱ele zu hoch geste̱ckt.

– sights
die Zi̱ele – goals

I don't see any **sign** of improvement.
Ich se̱he kein Ze̱ichen der Verbe̱sserung

sign – das Ze̱ichen

You gave no **sign** of having heard me.
Du hast kein Ze̱ichen gege̱ben, daß du
mich gehö̱rt hast.

sign – das Ze̱ichen

That's a/ bad/ good/ **sign**!
Das ist ein/ schle̱chtes/ gu̱tes/ Ze̱ichen!

sign – das Ze̱ichen

Silence is golden.
Schwe̱igen ist Gold.

silence – das Schwe̱igen

Stop this **silliness**!
Hör auf mit di̱eser A̱lbernheit!

silliness – die A̱lbernheit

Must you be so **silly**?
Mußt du so a̱lbern sein?

silly – a̱lbern

Silly me!
Wie kann ich so a̱lbern sein!

silly – a̱lbern

You're laughing yourself **silly**!
Du lachst dich kapṵtt!

– silly
kapṵtt – broken

It's so **simple**.
Es ist so e̱infach.

simple – e̱infach

159

SS SSS SS SSS SS SSS SS SSS SS SSS SS SSS SS SSS SS SSS

Don't say a **single** word!   *– single*
Sag kein einziges Wort!   einzig – only

My heart **sank**!   *– to sink*
Mein Herz ist mir in die Hose gerutscht!   rutschen – to slide

It hasn't **sunk in** yet.   to sink in – einsinken
Es ist mir noch nicht eingesunken.

Don't just **sit** there!   to sit – sitzen
Bleib bloß nicht da sitzen!

You're just **sitting** around.   *– sitting*
Du sitzt nur herum.   sitzen – to sit

What **size** are you?   size – die Größe
Welche Größe bist du?

That's about the **size** of it.   *– size*
Ja, so ungefähr kann man es sagen.   ungefähr – approximately

You're all **skin** and bones!   skin – die Haut
Du bist nur noch Haut und Knochen!

You missed by the **skin** of your teeth!   *– skin*
Du hast es hautdünn verpaßt.   hautdünn – as thin as skin

You're starting to get under my **skin**!   *– skin*
Du gehst mir langsam auf die Nerven!   die Nerven – nerves

I've been **slaving** over a hot stove all day!   to slave – sich plagen
Ich plage mich den ganzen Tag
am heißen Herd.

Sleep tight!   to sleep – schlafen
Schlaf gut!

SS SSS SS SSS SS SSS SS SSS SS SSS SS SSS SS SSS SS SSS SS SSS

I haven't **slept** a wink all night.   *– to sleep*
Ich habe die ganze Nacht kein Auge zugetan.   zutun – to close

I'll **sleep** on it.   to sleep on – überschlafen
Ich werde es mal überschlafen.

Don't lose any **sleep** over it.   sleep – der Schlaf
Verlier keinen Schlaf darüber!

Just let **sleeping** dogs lie.   sleeping – schlafend(e)
Schlafende Hunde soll man nicht wecken.

Do you have something up your **sleeve**?   *– sleeve*
Führst du etwas im Schilde?   das Schild – shield

You're letting things **slide**.   *– to slide*
Du läßt die Dinge laufen.   laufen – to run

Slip on/ off/ your coat!   *– to slip*
Zieht dir den Mantel an/aus.   an/ausziehen – to put on/off

Don't **slouch**.   *– to slouch*
Häng nicht so schlaff herum!   herumhängen – to hang around

We're making **slow** progress.   slow – langsam
Wir machen langsam Fortschritte.

Smoking is bad for you.   to smoke – rauchen
Rauchen ist schädlich für dich.

Try to **smooth** things **over**!   to smooth over – ausgleichen
Versuch, die Sachen auszugleichen!

Snack on fruit not candy.   to snack – naschen
Nasch lieber Obst, nicht Süßigkeiten!

SS SSS SS SSS SS SSS SS SSS SS SSS SS SSS SS SSS SS SSS

Snap out of it!   — *to snap*
Reiß dich zusammen!   (sich) zusammenreißen — to pull
                                                           oneself together

Make it **snappy**!   — *snappy*
Mach schnell!   schnell — fast

Don't **sneak off**!   to sneak off — davonschleichen
Schleich dich nicht davon!

It's not to be **sneezed at**.   — *to be sneezed at*
Es ist nicht zu verachten.   verachten — to scorn

You have the **sniffles**.   sniffles — der Schnupfen
Du hast einen leichten Schnupfen.

Be **so** kind and…   so — so
Sei so nett und....

So what do we do now?   so — also
Also, was machen wir jetzt?

You're **soaked** to the skin!   soaked — durchnäßt
Du bist bis auf die Haut durchnäßt!

You have a **soft** heart.   soft — weich(es)
Du hast ein weiches Herz.

There's **some** left; there are **some** left.   some — etwas
Es ist etwas übrig.

Give me **some**!   some — etwas
Gib mir etwas!

Do you want to be **somebody**?   — *somebody*
Willst du eine Persönlichkeit sein? die Persönlichkeit — personality

SS SSS SS SSS SS SSS SS SSS SS SSS SS SSS SS SSS SS SSS

Do you have **something** on your mind?   something – etwas
Hast du etwas im Sinn?

Did you do **something** behind my back?   something – etwas
Hast du etwas hinter meinem Rücken getan?

There's **something** about /him/ her/   something – etwas
I don't like.
Er/sie hat etwas an sich, was ich nicht mag.

There's **something** in what you say.   something – etwas
An dem, was du sagst, ist etwas dran.

Did you bring me **something** (little)?   something – etwas
Hast du mir etwas (kleines) gebracht?

Don't you have **something else** to do?   something (else) – etwas
Hast du nicht etwas anderes zu tun?   (anderes)

Why don't you go **somewhere** else?   somewhere – irgendwo
Warum gehst du nicht irgendwo anders hin?

As **soon** as possible.   soon – bald
So bald wie möglich.

It's too **soon** to tell.   *– soon*
Es ist zu früh zu sagen.   früh – early

Sooner or later.   *– sooner*
Früher oder später.   früher – earlier

I would sooner do it myself.   *– sooner*
Ich möchte es lieber selbst tun.   lieber – rather

You'll be **sorry**!   to be sorry – bereuen
Du wirst es bereuen.

163

SS SSS SS SSS SS SSS SS SSS SS SSS SS SSS SS SSS SS SSS

And you feel **sorry** for yourself.　　　　*– sorry*
Und du bemitleidest dich selbst.　　　sich bemitleiden – to feel
　　　　　　　　　　　　　　　　　　　　sorry for oneself

Sort of.　　　　　　　　　　　　sort of – irgendwie
Irgendwie

You seem to be out of **sorts**.　　　　　*– sorts*
Du scheinst verstimmt zu sein.　　　verstimmt – upset

It **sounds** (seems) like a good idea.　　to sound – sich anhören
Das hört sich an wie eine gute Idee.

How does that **sound** (seem) to you?　　　*– to sound*
Wie findest du das?　　　　　　　finden – to find

It **sounds** like trouble.　　　　　　　*– to sound*
Es können Schwierigkeiten kommen.　　kommen – to come

By the sound of it, you're annoyed.　　　*– by the sound of it*
Wie es sich anhört, bist du verärgert.　sich anhören – to sound

That bike takes up a lot of **space**.　　　space – der Platz
Das Fahrrad nimmt viel Platz ein.

Watch for a **parking space**!　　(parking) space – der Parkplatz
Paß auf einen Parkplatz auf!

This room is cramped for **space**.　　　　*– space*
Dieses Zimmer ist räumlich beschränkt.　beschränkt – cramped

I'm going to give you a **spanking**.　　　　*– spanking*
Ich werde dir den Hintern versohlen.　versohlen – to tan

Spare (save) me the details!　　　　to spare – verschonen
Verschone mich mit den Einzelheiten!

164

SS SSS SS SSS SS SSS SS SSS SS SSS SS SSS SS SSS SS SSS SS SSS

You tried to **spare** your friend's feelings.
Du hast an die Gefühle deines Freundes
gedacht.

– to spare
denken – to think

I have no time to **spare**.
Ich habe keine Zeit übrig.

– to spare
übrig – left over

What are you doing in our **spare time**?
Was machst du in unserer Freizeit?

– spare time
die Freizeit – free time

I'll **speak** to him about it.
Ich werde mit ihm darüber sprechen.

to speak – sprechen

Speak for yourself!
Äußere nur deine eigene Meinung!

– to speak
äußern – to express

Speak up!
Mach den Mund auf!

– to speak up
aufmachen – to open

What's so **special** about it?
Was ist denn so besonders daran?

special – besonders

Could you be more **specific**?
Kannst du dich etwas genauer äußern?

specific – genau

How do you **spell** it?
Wie buchstabiert man es?

to spell – buchstabieren

Do I have to **spell** it out for you?
Muß ich mit dir noch deutlicher werden?

– to spell
deutlicher – more clearly

It **spells** disaster!
Das bedeutet Schwierigkeiten!

– to spell
bedeuten – to mean

You **spend** money like water.
Du gibst Geld aus, als ob es Wasser wäre.

to spend – ausgeben

165

SS SSS SS SSS SS SSS SS SSS SS SSS SS SSS SS SSS SS SSS

Watch he doesn't take a **spill**! *– spill*
Paß auf, daß er nicht fällt! fallen – to fall

That's the **spirit**! *– spirit*
Das ist die richtige Einstellung! die Einstellung – attitude

You're the **spitting image** of your father! spitting image –
Du bist das genaue Ebenbild deines Vaters! das Ebenbild

You're **splitting hairs**. *– to split hairs*
Du treibst Haarspalterei. die Haarspalterei – hair-splitting

You are **spoiled**. spoiled – verwöhnt
Du bist verwöhnt.

Be a good **sport**! *– sport*
Mach schön mit! mitmachen – to participate

You're **squinting**. to squint – schielen
Du schielst.

Don't **squirt/ Squirt** the water. to squirt – spritzen
Spritz nicht/Spritz mit dem Wasser!

I'd **stake** my life on it! *– to stake*
Ich würde meine Hand dafür ins Feuer legen. legen – to place

Stop **stalling for time**! to stall for time – Zeit gewinnen
Hör auf zu versuchen, Zeit zu gewinnen!

Stop **stamping your feet**. *– to stamp your feet*
Stell das Fußstampfen ein! das Fußstampfen – foot-stamping

I can't **stand** her. to stand – ausstehen
Ich kann sie nicht ausstehen.

SS SSS SS SSS SS SSS SS SSS SS SSS SS SSS SS SSS SS SSS SS SSS

Don't just **stand** there!
Steh nicht bloß herum!

to stand – stehen

You can't **stand** the sight of blood!
Ich kann Blut nicht sehen.

– *to stand*
sehen – to see

You've got to **stand your ground**.
Du mußt deinen Standpunkt
vertreten!

–to stand one's ground
den Standpunkt vertreten –
to represent one's point of view

It **stands to reason** that…
Es ist logisch, daß....

– to stand to reason
logisch – logical

The answer was **staring you in the face**!
Die Antwort lag klar auf der Hand!

– to stare in the face
auf der Hand liegen –
to lie on the hand

Let's **start** by making the bed.
Fangen wir damit an, das Bett zu machen.

to start – anfangen

Let's get **started**.
Fangen wir an!

to start – anfangen

Now don't you **start**!
Fang auch nicht du damit an!

to start – anfangen

You're just a slow **starter**.
Du bist nur ein Spätentwickler.

– starter
der Spätentwickler – a late developer

I'm **starving**!
Ich komme vor Hunger fast um!

– to starve
umkommen – to die

Stay where you are!
Bleib, wo du bist!

to stay – bleiben

167

SS SSS SS SSS SS SSS SS SSS SS SSS SS SSS SS SSS SS SSS

Stay out of this!   *– to stay out of*
Misch dich hier nicht ein!   sich einmischen – to interfere

Go to your room and let off some **steam**.   (to let off) steam –
Geh in dein Zimmer und   Dampf ablassen
laß etwas Dampf ab!

You'd better watch your **step**.   *– step*
Du sollst vorsichtig sein.   vorsichtig – cautious

Stick 'em up!   *– to stick 'em up*
Hände hoch!   hoch – high

Don't **stick** your tongue **out** at me!   to stick out – herausstrecken
Streck mir die Zunge nicht heraus!

Stick to the facts!   *– to stick to*
Bleib bei den Tatsachen!   bleiben – to remain

Stick to your guns!   *– to stick to one's guns*
Bleib deiner Sache treu!   treubleiben – to remain faithful to

Your hair is **sticking up**.   to be sticking up – abstehen
Dein Haar steht ab.

I don't need you to **stir things up**.   *– to stir things up*
Ich brauche nicht, daß du Unruhe stiftest.   Unruhe stiften –
                         to cause unrest

A **stitch** in time saves nine.   *– stitch*
Was du heute kannst besorgen, das   besorgen –
verschiebe nicht auf morgen!   to take care of

You can't play on an empty **stomach**.   stomach – der Magen
Du kannst mit leerem Magen nicht spielen.

168

SS SSS SS SSS SS SSS SS SSS SS SSS SS SSS SS SSS SS SSS SS SSS

Stop jumping up and down (on the sofa).   to stop – <u>au</u>fhören
Hör auf dam<u>i</u>t, (auf dem S<u>o</u>fa) 'rauf und 'r<u>u</u>nter zu spr<u>i</u>ngen!

Stop what you're doing and listen to me.   to stop – <u>au</u>fhören
Hör auf dam<u>i</u>t und hör mir zu!

Don't **stop** short.   to stop – <u>au</u>fhören
Hör nicht zu früh auf!

This has got to **stop**!   – *to stop*
Das muß ein <u>E</u>nde h<u>a</u>ben!   das <u>E</u>nde – end

I'm putting a **stop** to that.   – *stop*
Ich m<u>a</u>che d<u>ie</u>ser S<u>a</u>che ein <u>E</u>nde.   das <u>E</u>nde – end

Pull out all the **stops**!   – *stops*
Zieh <u>a</u>lle Reg<u>i</u>ster!   das Reg<u>i</u>ster – register

It's the **story** of your life!   – *story*
Es ist für dich <u>i</u>mmer   das Pr<u>o</u>blem – problem
das gl<u>ei</u>che Pr<u>o</u>blem!

How can you keep a **straight** face?   – *straight*
Wie kannst du ein <u>e</u>rnstes Ges<u>i</u>cht   ernst(es) – serious
bew<u>a</u>hren?

Get **straight** to the point!   – *straight*
Komm gleich zur S<u>a</u>che!   gleich – right away

Come **straight** out with it!   – *straight*
Sag es mir ganz <u>o</u>ffen!   <u>o</u>ffen – openly

Straighten your room.   to straighten – <u>au</u>fräumen
Räum dein Z<u>i</u>mmer auf!

SS SSS SS SSS SS SSS SS SSS SS SSS SS SSS SS SSS SS SSS

You'll **strain** your eyes.   to strain – über**a**nstrengen
Du wirst dir die A**u**gen über**a**nstrengen.

You seem to be under a lot of **strain**.   – *strain*
Du scheinst unter viel Druck zu sein.   der Druck – pressure

Why are you giving me a **strange** look?   strange – k**o**misch
War**u**m siehst du mich so k**o**misch an?

That's the last **straw**!   – *straw*
Das ist der G**i**pfel!   der G**i**pfel – peak

Let's **stretch** our legs!   to stretch – vertr**e**ten
Vertr**e**ten wir uns mal die B**ei**ne!

I think you're **stretching** the truth.   – *to stretch*
Du nimmst die W**a**hrheit nicht **a**llzu gen**au**.   gen**au** – exactly

I'm not being too **strict**!   strict – streng
Ich bin nicht streng gen**u**g!

Be home at the **stroke** of five!   – *stroke*
Sei Punkt fünf Uhr zu H**au**se!   der Punkt – dot

You're as **stubborn** as a mule!   stubborn – st**ö**rrisch
Du bist so st**ö**rrisch wie ein M**au**lesel!

Of all the **stupid** things to do!   stupid – dumm
Wie kann man so 'was D**u**mmes m**a**chen!

You're very much in **style.**   style – die M**o**de
Du bist sehr in M**o**de.

Such is life!   such – so
So ist das L**e**ben.

170

SS SSS SS SSS SS SSS SS SSS SS SSS SS SSS SS SSS SS SSS SS SSS

Did you ever see **such** a thing!　　　　such – so
Hast du jemals so etwas gesehen?

I **suggest** we discuss this tomorrow.　　to suggest – vorschlagen
Ich schlage vor, wir besprechen es morgen.

Suit yourself!　　　　　　　　– *to suit*
Wie du willst!　　　　　　　wollen – to want

That **suits** me fine!　　　　　　– *to suit*
Das ist mir recht!　　　　　　recht – okay

Don't **sulk**!　　　　　　　to sulk – schmollen
Schmoll nicht!

Why are you **sulking**?　　　　to sulk – schmollen
Warum schmollst du?

Get dressed in your **Sunday** best!　　Sunday – der Sonntag
Zieh deine Sonntagskleider an!

I **suppose**/ so/ not/.　　　　　– *to suppose*
Ich glaube/ schon/ kaum/.　　glauben – to believe

I don't **suppose** you'd consider　　　– *to suppose*
sharing your ice cream (with me).　　glauben – to believe
Ich glaube kaum, daß du (mit mir) dein Eis teilst.

The book is **supposed** to be pretty good.　be supposed to – sollen
Das Buch soll ziemlich gut sein.

You're not **supposed** to go out.　　be supposed to – sollen
Du sollst nicht hinausgehen!

You were **supposed** to make your bed.　be supposed to – sollen
Du hättest dein Bett machen sollen.

171

You're very **sure** of yourself!	sure – sicher
Du bist deiner Sache sehr sicher!	

I **sure** am! You bet! **Sure** thing!	sure – sicher
Ganz sicher!	

Make sure you come home on time!	*– to make sure*
Vergiß nicht, rechtzeitig nach Hause	vergessen – to forget
zu kommen!	

You're in for a **surprise**!	surprise – die Überraschung
Du wirst eine Überraschung erleben!	

It didn't come as much of a **surprise**.	surprise – die Überraschung
Das war keine Überraschung.	

I shouldn't be **surprised**.	to be surprised – überrascht
Ich soll nicht überrascht sein.	

Swearing is naughty!	swearing – das Fluchen
Fluchen ist ungezogen!	

That's very **sweet** of you.	sweet – lieb
Das ist sehr lieb von dir.	

Switch places with him.	to switch – tauschen
Tausch mit ihm die Plätze!	

T

That's you to a **T**!
Genau so bist du.

I'm keeping **tabs** on you.
Ich beh<u>a</u>lte dich gen<u>au</u> im <u>Au</u>ge.

– *tabs*
das <u>Au</u>ge – eye

Take the day off!
Nimm dir den Tag frei!

to take – n<u>e</u>hmen

Take it or leave it!
Die Entsch<u>ei</u>dung liegt bei dir.

– *to take*
die Entsch<u>ei</u>dung – decision

TTT TT TTT TT TTT TT TTT TT TTT TT TTT TT TTT TT

How long does this **take**?	– *to take*
Wie lange dauert es?	dauern – to last
It won't **take** long.	– *to take*
Es dauert nicht lange.	dauern – to last
You always **take apart** your toys.	to take apart – zerlegen
Du zerlegst immer deine Spielsachen.	
Take the balls **out** of the car!	to take out – nehmen aus
Nimm die Bälle aus dem Wagen!	
Don't **take** it **out on** me!	– *to take out on*
Laß deinen Zorn nicht an mir aus!	auslassen – to let out
You always **take** his/ her **side**!	– *to take sides*
Du stehst immer auf seiner/ihrer Seite!	stehen – to stand
You're a fine one to **talk**!	to talk – reden
(Look who's talking!)	
Schau mal, wer redet!	
I might as well be **talking** to the wall!	to talk – reden
Ich könnte besser gegen den Wind reden!	
I don't want to **talk** about it.	to talk – sprechen
Ich will nicht darüber sprechen.	
I could hear you **talking**.	to talk – sprechen
Ich konnte dich sprechen hören.	
I don't know what you're **talking** about.	to talk – sprechen
Ich habe keine Ahnung, worüber du sprichst.	
I realize I'm **talking** to myself.	– *to talk*
Es ist mir klar, ich führe Selbstgespräche.	führen – to lead

TTT TT TTT TT TTT TT TTT TT TTT TT TTT TT TTT TT

You're **talking** to yourself.
Du führst Selbstgespräche.

– to talk
führen – to lead

Now you're **talking**!
Das läßt sich schon eher hören!

– to talk
hören – to hear

Don't **talk back** to me!
Ich möchte keine Widersprüche
haben.

– to talk back
die Widersprüche –
contradictions

Don't let her/ him **talk** you **into** it.
Laß nicht, daß er/sie es dir einredet!

to talk into – einreden

Don't let/ her/ him/ **talk** you **out of** it.
Laß nicht, daß/ er/ sie/ es dir ausredet!

to talk out of – ausreden

I'm going to give you a real **talking to**!
Ich werde dir ins Gewissen reden!   das Gewissen – the conscience

– to talk to

That's a **tall order**.
Das ist starke Zumutung!

– tall order
die Zumutung – demand

Your hair is all **tangled**.
Dein Haar ist ganz verknotet.

tangled – verknotet

It takes two to **tango**!
Es gibt immer zwei Seiten!

– to tango
die Seite – side

Who's **tapping** me on the shoulder?
Wer klopft mir auf die Schulter?

to tap – klopfen

There's no accounting for **taste**.
Über Geschmack läßt sich nicht streiten.

taste – der Geschmack

That'll **teach** you!
Das hast du nun davon!

– to teach
davon – from it

TTT TT TTT TT TTT TT TTT TT TTT TT TTT TT TTT TT

Tear yourself **away** from your   to tear away – <u>lo</u>sreißen
game, and come and eat.
Reiß dich von d<u>ei</u>nem Sp<u>ie</u>l los und komm zum <u>E</u>ssen!

I'm **tearing** my hair **out**!   to tear out – <u>au</u>sreißen
Ich r<u>ei</u>ße mir die H<u>aa</u>re aus.

I was only **teasing**!   to tease – r<u>ei</u>zen
Ich w<u>o</u>llte dich nur r<u>ei</u>zen.

You're **telling** me!   to tell, say – s<u>a</u>gen
Wem sagst du das!

Tell the truth!   to tell, say – s<u>a</u>gen
Sag die W<u>a</u>hrheit!

Do as I **tell** you, or else!   to tell, say – s<u>a</u>gen
Tu, was ich dir s<u>a</u>ge, sonst gibt's Krach!

I may **tell** you and I may not.   to tell, say – s<u>a</u>gen
Viell<u>ei</u>cht s<u>a</u>ge ich es dir, und viell<u>ei</u>cht nicht.

You mustn't **tell** anyone!   to tell, say – s<u>a</u>gen
Du sollst es n<u>ie</u>mandem s<u>a</u>gen!

I **told** you so!   to tell, say – s<u>a</u>gen
Ich h<u>a</u>be es dir ja ges<u>a</u>gt!

Do as you're **told**!   to tell, say – s<u>a</u>gen
Tu, was man dir sagt!

I've **told** you before!   to tell, say – s<u>a</u>gen
Ich h<u>a</u>be es dir schon mal ges<u>a</u>gt!

You were **told** to do it.   to tell, say – s<u>a</u>gen
Es w<u>u</u>rde dir ges<u>a</u>gt, es zu tun.

176

TTT TT TTT TT TTT TT TTT TT TTT TT TTT TT TTT TT

I can't **tell** if you're sad or not.
Ich kann nicht wissen, ob du
traurig bist oder nicht.

– to tell
wissen – to know

There's no **telling** what you'll do next!
Man kann nicht wissen, was du
demnächst machst.

– to tell
wissen – to know

You never can **tell**.
Man kann nie wissen.

– to tell
wissen – to know

How can you **tell**?
Woher soll man wissen?

– to tell
wissen – to know

I can't **tell** the difference.
Ich kann nicht unterscheiden.

– to tell
unterscheiden – to differentiate

I'm not asking you; I'm **telling** you!
Ich bitte dich nicht; ich
verlange es von dir!

– to tell
verlangen – to demand

Hold your **temper**!
Beherrsch dich!

– temper
sich beherrschen – to control oneself

You're a **terror**!
Du bist ein Schrecken!

terror – der Schrecken

You need an eye **test**.
Du brauchst eine Augenuntersuchung.

test – die Untersuchung

That's it for today.
Das reicht für heute.

that – das

That's right!
Das stimmt!

that – das

177

TTT TT TTT TT TTT TT TTT TT TTT TT TTT TT TTT TT

That will do!
Das reicht!

that – das

That's strange!
Das ist komisch!

that – das

That's that!
Das wär's!

that – das

That's enough of that!
Das ist genug!

that – das

You've got me **there**!
Da bin ich überfragt!

there – da

There were things lying all about.
Da lagen die Sachen überall herum.

there – da

What's that **thing**?
Was ist das für ein Ding?

thing – das Ding

They are one and the same **thing**.
Die sind beide dasselbe.

– *thing*
dasselbe – the same thing

I don't know a **thing** about it.
Davon weiß ich gar nichts.

– *thing*
davon – about it

There is no such **thing**.
So etwas gibt es nicht.

– *thing*
etwas – something

It's just one of the **things**.
So etwas kommt eben vor.

– *thing*
etwas – something

You've got to **think** straight.
Man muß klar denken.

to think – denken

TTT TT TTT TT TTT TT TTT TT TTT TT TTT TT TTT TT

Did you **think** to bring along something to eat?	to think – d<u>e</u>nken
Hast du dar<u>a</u>n ged<u>a</u>cht, <u>e</u>twas zu <u>e</u>ssen m<u>i</u>tzubringen?	

I can't **think** of everything.   to think – d<u>e</u>nken
Ich kann nicht an <u>a</u>lles d<u>e</u>nken.

You've got another **think** coming!   to think – d<u>e</u>nken
Das hast du dir wohl ged<u>a</u>cht!

I **thought** as much.   to think – d<u>e</u>nken
Das h<u>a</u>be ich mir ged<u>a</u>cht.

I **thought** we'd have a chat.   to think – d<u>e</u>nken
Ich h<u>a</u>be ged<u>a</u>cht, wir k<u>ö</u>nnten m<u>i</u>teinander spr<u>e</u>chen.

I don't **think** much of the idea.   to think – h<u>a</u>lten
Ich h<u>a</u>lte nicht viel von der Id<u>ee</u>.

That's what *you* **think**!   to think – m<u>ei</u>nen
Das meinst du!

I can't **think** of an answer.   *– to think*
Ich k<u>o</u>mme nicht auf <u>ei</u>ne <u>A</u>ntwort!   k<u>o</u>mmen – to come

Think/ Plan ahead!   *– to think*
Pl<u>a</u>ne im vor<u>au</u>s!   pl<u>a</u>nen – to plan

Now that I come to **think** of it...   *– to think*
Wenn ich es mir jetzt überl<u>e</u>ge....   überl<u>e</u>gen – to consider

I'd **think** twice about that, if I were you.   *– to think*
Ich w<u>ü</u>rde es mir zw<u>ei</u>mal überl<u>e</u>gen,   überl<u>e</u>gen – to consider
wenn ich in d<u>ei</u>ner Haut st<u>e</u>ckte.

TTT TT TTT TT TTT TT TTT TT TTT TT TTT TT TTT TT

Think what we could do with all   *– to think*
that money!   überlegen – to consider
Überleg's dir, was wir mit
dem ganzen Geld machen könnten!

You did it without **thinking**.   *– to think*
Du hast unüberlegt gehandelt.   unüberlegt – without thinking

I'll **think** it **over**.   to think over – nachdenke
Ich denke mal darüber nach.

Don't give it another **thought**!   thought – der Gedanke
Mach dir keine Gedanken mehr darüber!

You look lost in **thought**.   thought – der Gedanke
Du scheinst, in Gedanken versunken zu sein.

I've got to get my **thoughts** together.   thoughts – die Gedanken
Ich muß meine Gedanken zusammenbringen.

I'm **thrilled** for you!   *– thrilled*
Ich freue mich riesig für dich!   sich freuen – to be happy

There's no need to jump down my **throat**.   *– throat*
Es gibt keinen Grund, mich anzufahren!   anfahren – to yell at

You're always at each other's **throats**!   *– throat*
Ihr liegt Euch immer in den Haaren!   die Haare – hair

You're finally sleeping the whole   through – durch
night **through**.
Endlich schläfst du die ganze Nacht durch.

You're all **thumbs**!   *– thumb*
Du hast zwei linke Hände.   die Hände – hands

TTT TT TTT TT TTT TT TTT TT TTT TT TTT TT TTT TT

Give a **thumbs** up!   – *thumb*
Gib mir ein Zeichen, daß alles   das Zeichen – sign
in Ordnung ist.

Give a **thumbs** down!   – *thumb*
Gib mir ein Zeichen, daß alles verkehrt ist.   das Zeichen – sign

It was just the **ticket**!   – *ticket*
Es war genau das Richtige!   das Richtige – the right thing

Are you **ticklish**?   ticklish – kitzelig
Bist du kitzelig?

I've got a thing about **tidiness**.   tidiness – die Ordentlichkeit
Ich habe einen richtigen Fimmel mit Ordentlichkeit.

Money's a bit **tight** at the moment.   tight – knapp
Das Geld ist im Moment knapp.

Tilt your head backwards/forwards.   – *to tilt*
Leg den Kopf nach hinten/nach vorn!   legen – to lay, place

It's high **time**!   time – die Zeit
Es ist höchste Zeit!

There's no **time** for that!   time – die Zeit
Es gibt dafür keine Zeit!

All in good **time**.   time – die Zeit
Alles mit der Zeit.

There's a **time** and place for everything.   time – die Zeit
Alles hat seine Zeit.

You have a lot of **time** on your hands.   time – die Zeit
Du hast viel freie Zeit.

181

TTT TT TTT TT TTT TT TTT TT TTT TT TTT TT TTT TT

When I have **time**.   time – die Zeit
Wenn ich Zeit habe.

Driving you to practice takes a great time – die Zeit
deal of my **time**.
Wenn ich dich zum Training fahre,
nimmt es viel von meiner Zeit in Anspruch.

It takes **time**.   time – die Zeit
Es braucht Zeit.

Time's up!   time – die Zeit
Die Zeit ist abgelaufen!

Time will tell.   time – die Zeit
Es wird sich mit der Zeit herausstellen.

Time is money.   time – die Zeit
Zeit ist Geld.

You took your **time**!   time – die Zeit
Du hast dir Zeit gelassen!

For the **time** being.   *– time*
Vorübergehend. vorübergehend – for the time being

Time and **time** again!   *– time*
Immer wieder!   wieder – again

Well **timed**!   *– timed*
Du hast genau den richtigen der Zeitpunkt – point in time
Zeitpunkt ausgesucht!

Badly **timed**!   *– timed*
Du hast einen schlechten der Zeitpunkt – point in time
Zeitpunkt ausgesucht!

TTT TT TTT TT TTT TT TTT TT TTT TT TTT TT TTT TT

Just a **tiny** bit.
Nur ein kleines bißchen.

tiny bit – kleines bißchen

I have it on the **tip** of my tongue!
Es liegt mir auf der Zunge!

– *tip*
die Zunge – tongue

You look kind of **tired**.
Du siehst etwas müde aus.

tired – müde

Have you lost your **tongue**?
Hast du die Sprache verloren?

– *tongue*
die Sprache – speech

I'll not **tolerate** such conduct!
Ein solches Benehmen dulde ich nicht.

to tolerate – dulden

Too much food is bad for you.
Zuviel Essen ist schädlich für dich.

too – zu

Too bad. (problem)
Wie schade.

too
wie – how

Eye for an eye, a tooth for a **tooth**.
Auge um Auge, Zahn um Zahn.

tooth – der Zahn

You're shouting at the **top** of
your voice!
Du schreist aus Leibeskräften!

– *top*
die Leibeskräfte – with all one's might

You'll come out **on top**.
Du wirst die Oberhand gewinnen.

– *(on) top*
die Oberhand – upper hand

Toss me the newspaper!
Wirf mir die Zeitung zu!

to toss – werfen

I'm a soft **touch**. (money)
Ich bin nachgiebig.

– *touch*
nachgiebig – yielding, soft

183

TTT TT TTT TT TTT TT TTT TT TTT TT TTT TT TTT TT

I'm **touched**.   touched – berührt
Ich bin berührt.

Don't be so **touchy**!   touchy, sensitive – empfindlich
Sei nicht so empfindlich!

Eating is a **touchy** subject.   touchy – heikel, heikl--
Essen ist ein heikles Thema.

You're a real **tough** guy!   tough – zäh
Du bist ein zäher Bursche!

I've lost **track** of time.   track – der Überblick
Ich habe den Überblick über die Zeit verloren.

Trade places with your brother!   to trade – tauschen
Tausch die Plätze mit deinem Bruder!

You've got a real **treat** in store.   – treat
Du bekommst etwas, worauf du   sich freuen – to be pleased
dich freuen kannst.

You **treat** your room like a hotel!   – to treat
Du hältst dein Zimmer wie ein   halten – to keep
Hotelraum!

It's my **treat**!   – treat
Das geht auf meine Kosten!   die Kosten – costs

Sometimes school is a real **trial**!   – trial
Manchmal kann die Schule eine   die Plage – nuisance
wahre Plage sein!

That should do the **trick**!   – trick
Das müßte eigentlich klappen!   klappen – to succeed

TTT TT TTT TT TTT TT TTT TT TTT TT TTT TT TTT TT

You know all the **tricks**!
Du bist in allen Wassern gewaschen!

– tricks
waschen – to wash

It's a **tricky** situation.
Es ist eine heikle Situation.

tricky – heikel, heikl--

Don't make **trouble**!
Mach keinen Ärger!

– trouble
der Ärger – aggravation, anger

What seems to be the **trouble**?
Was ist denn los?

– trouble
los – wrong, loose

It's more **trouble** that it's worth.
Das ist nicht der Mühe wert.

– trouble
die Mühe – the effort

Keep out of **trouble**!
Gerate nicht in Schwierigkeiten!

trouble(s) – die Schwierigkeiten

How **true**!
Das ist schon wahr!

true – wahr

I **trust** you.
Ich habe Vertrauen zu dir.

trust – das Vertrauen

There's no harm in **trying**.
Es kann nicht schaden, es zu versuchen.

to try – versuchen

You can always **try**.
Man kann immer versuchen.

to try – versuchen

Just you **try**!
Versuch es mal!

to try – versuchen

Try your hand at golf!
Versuch mal Golf!

to try – versuchen

185

You're **trying** very hard.	*– to try*
Du gibst dir viel Mühe.	die Mühe – effort

Could you have **tried** harder?	*– to try*
Konntest du dir nicht mehr Mühe machen?	die Mühe – effort

You didn't really **try**.	*– to try*
Du hast dir überhaupt keine Mühe gemacht.	die Mühe – effort

It's worth a **try**.	try – der Versuch
Es ist einen Versuch wert.	

I'll **tuck** you **in**.	*to tuck in*
Ich werde dich zudecken.	zudecken – to cover over

Take turns on the swing!	(to take) turns – abwechselnd
Spielt abwechselnd auf der Schaukel!	

One good **turn** deserves another.	*– turn*
Eine Hand wäscht die andere.	waschen – to wash

Turn it down! (volume)	to turn down –
Stell es bitte leiser!	leiser stellen

It's time to **turn over** a new leaf.	*– to turn over*
Es ist Zeit, einen neuen Anfang zu machen.	der Anfang – the beginning

Turn up your collar!	to turn up – hochklappen
Klapp den Kragen hoch!	

Something is sure to **turn up**.	*– to turn up*
Etwas wird passieren.	passieren – to happen

U

Your Dad and I are still **undecided**.   undecided – u̠nentschlossen
Dein Va̠ter und ich sind noch u̠nentschlossen.

You're still **under-age**.   under-age – mi̠nderjährig
Du bist noch mi̠nderjährig.

You'll **understand** one day.   to understand – verste̠hen
Du wirst e̠ines Ta̠ges verste̠hen.

The buttons have come **undone**.   undone – a̠ufgegangen
Die Knö̠pfe sind a̠ufgegangen.

UU UUU UU UUU UU UUU UU UUU UU UUU UU UUU UU

It was **unintentional**.
Das war <u>o</u>hne <u>A</u>bsicht.

unintentional – <u>o</u>hne <u>A</u>bsicht

You look **unkempt**.
Du siehst <u>u</u>ngekämmt aus.

unkempt – <u>u</u>ngekämmt

It's **unlike** you to do such a thing.
Es paßt nicht zu dir, so <u>e</u>twas zu
m<u>a</u>chen.

– unlike
p<u>a</u>ssen – to to match

You're being **unreasonable**.
Du verl<u>a</u>ngst zuv<u>ie</u>l.

– unreasonable
verl<u>a</u>ngen – to demand

It's better left **unsaid**.
Es ist b<u>e</u>sser, es zu verschw<u>ei</u>gen.

– unsaid
verschw<u>ei</u>gen – to conceal

That chair is a little **unsteady**.
Der Stuhl ist <u>e</u>twas w<u>a</u>ckelig.

unsteady – w<u>a</u>ckelig

The film is **unsuitable** for children.
Der Film ist für K<u>i</u>nder nicht ge<u>ei</u>gnet.

unsuitable – nicht ge<u>ei</u>gnet

Your room is so **untidy**.
Dein Z<u>i</u>mmer ist so <u>u</u>nordentlich.

untidy – <u>u</u>nordentlich

You've left your meal **untouched**.
Du hast dein <u>E</u>ssen nicht ber<u>ü</u>hrt.

untouched – nicht ber<u>ü</u>hrt

Something's **up**.
Da stimmt <u>e</u>twas nicht.

– up
st<u>i</u>mmen – to be right

It's **up to** you to do it.
Es liegt an dir, ob du es machst.

– up to
l<u>ie</u>gen – to lie

UU UUU UU UUU UU UUU UU UUU UU UUU UU UUU UU

I don't feel **up to** it.
Ich fühle mich dem nicht gewachsen.

to be up to – gewachsen

What are **you up** to?
Was hast du vor?

to be up to – vorhaben

Are you **up to** something?
Hast du etwas im Sinn?

– *to be up to*
der Sinn – mind

Don't get **uppity**!
Werde nicht hochnäsig!

uppity – hochnäsig

What's the **use** of worrying?
Was nützt es, sich Sorgen zu machen?

to be of use – nützen

It's no **use** crying.
Es hat keinen Sinn zu weinen.

– *to be of use*
der Sinn – sense

You could **use** some sleep.
Du könntest etwas Schlaf gebrauchen.

to use – gebrauchen

It will come in **useful**.
Es könnte sich als nützlich erweisen.

useful – nützlich

Make yourself **useful**!
Mach dich nützlich!

useful – nützlich

You're not your **usual**/ cheery/
thoughtful/ self today.
Du bist heute nicht so/ munter/ nachdenklich/ wie sonst.

usual – sonst

It's not **usual** for you to be this late.
Du kommst normalerweise nicht
so spät.

– *usual*
normalerweise – normally

UU UUU UU UUU UU UUU UU UUU UU UUU UU UUU

Do you want to play/checkers/ chess/ ?
Willst du /Dame/ Schach/ spielen?
Vihlst doo /DAH-meh/ schasch/ SHPEE-l'n?

Whose turn is it?
Wer ist dran ?
Vehr ihst dran?

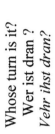

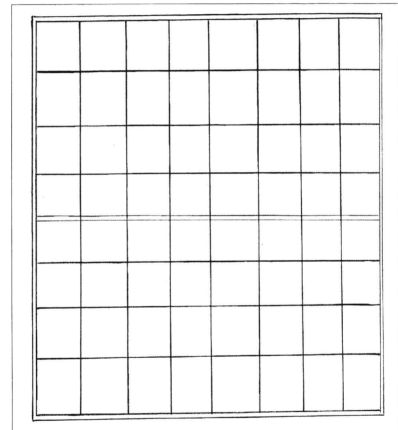

You aren't playing fairly.
Du spielst nicht fair!
Doo shpeelst nihsht fair!

VW

For the sake of **variety**....
Zur Abwechslung.....

variety – die Abwechslung

Eat your **vegetables**!
Iß dein Gemüse!

vegetables – das Gemüse

Vent your feelings!
Laß deinen Gefühlen freien Lauf!

– *to vent*
lassen – to allow

Nothing **ventured** nothing gained.
Wer nicht wagt, der nicht gewinnt.

– *to venture*
wagen – to risk

VW VW VW VW VW VW VW VW VW VW VW VW VW

Listen to the **voice** of reason!   *– voice*
Nimm doch Vern<u>u</u>nft an!   die Vern<u>u</u>nft – reason

You're shouting at the top of your **voice**!   *– voice*
Du schreist aus L<u>ei</u>beskräften!   schr<u>ei</u>en – to shout

He waddles like a duck when he   to waddle – w<u>a</u>tscheln
dances!
Er w<u>a</u>tschelt wie <u>ei</u>ne <u>E</u>nte, wenn er tanzt!

Wait and see.   to wait – <u>a</u>bwarten
Mal <u>a</u>bwarten!

Wait for the right moment!   to wait – w<u>a</u>rten
W<u>a</u>rte auf den r<u>i</u>chtigen Mom<u>e</u>nt!

I don't want you to **walk** home alone.   to walk – g<u>e</u>hen
Ich will nicht, daß du all<u>ei</u>n nach H<u>au</u>se gehst.

You just can't **walk away** from trouble.   *– to walk away*
Schw<u>ie</u>rigkeiten muß man <u>a</u>nfassen.   <u>a</u>nfassen – to tackle

You really **want** that doll badly.   to want – m<u>ö</u>chten
Du m<u>ö</u>chtest d<u>ie</u>se P<u>u</u>ppe w<u>i</u>rklich h<u>a</u>ben.

Anything you **want**.   to want – w<u>o</u>llen
Was <u>i</u>mmer du willst.

What do you **want** with him?   to want – w<u>o</u>llen
Was willst du mit ihm?

That's the last thing we **want**!   to want – w<u>o</u>llen
Das ist das allerl<u>e</u>tzte, was wir w<u>o</u>llen!

192

VW VW VW VW VW VW VW VW VW VW VW VW VW

You're getting **warmer**! (Game)
Es wird schon wärmer!

warm – warm

You could have **warned** me!
Du hast mich warnen können!

to warn – warnen

You have been **warned**!
Du bist gewarnt worden!

to warn – warnen

Wash the tub thoroughly!
Wasch die Badewanne gründlich!

to wash – waschen

Your jeans are being **washed**
(in the wash).
Deine Jeans werden gewaschen.

to wash – waschen

Waste not want not.
Spare in der Zeit, so hast du in der Not.

– to waste
sparen – to save

Watch your language!
Paß auf deine Aussprache auf!

to watch – aufpassen

That's all **water** under the bridge.
Das gehört längst zur
Vergangenheit.

– water
die Vergangenheit – the past

Your argument doesn't hold **water**.
Dieses Argument ist nicht stichhaltig.

– water
stichhaltig – valid, conclusive

Don't bother turning on the **waterworks**!
Es hat keinen Zweck, Tränen zu vergießen!

– waterworks
die Tranen – tears

Don't **wave** the knife around!
Schwing nicht drohend mit dem Messer umher!

to wave – schwingen

VW VW VW VW VW VW VW VW VW VW VW VW VW

You'll find a **way** of doing it.   way – der Weg
Du wirst schon <u>ei</u>nen Weg f<u>i</u>nden, es zu tun.

Don't stand in my **way**.   way – der Weg
Steh mir nicht im Weg!

Keep out of the **way**.   way – der Weg
Bleib aus dem Weg!

You're **in the way**.   (in the) way – der Weg
Du bist im Weg.

Get **out of the way**!   (out of the) way – der Weg
Geh aus dem Weg!

No **way**!   – *way*
<u>Au</u>sgeschlossen!   <u>au</u>sgeschlossen – out of the question

One **way** or another...   – *way*
So oder so.....   so – so

You have a **way** with numbers/ words.   – *way*
Du verst<u>e</u>hst es, mit   verst<u>e</u>hen – to understand
Z<u>a</u>hlen/W<u>ö</u>rtern <u>u</u>mzugehen.

Lead the **way**!   – *way*
Geh vor<u>a</u>n!   vor<u>a</u>n – ahead

I can't look the other **way**.   – *way*
Ich kann nicht w<u>e</u>gsehen.   w<u>e</u>gsehen – to look away

Why won't you **wear** it?   to wear – tr<u>a</u>gen
War<u>u</u>m willst du es nicht tr<u>a</u>gen?

VW VW VW VW VW VW VW VW VW VW VW VW VW

That story (excuse) is **wearing** thin.
Die Geschichte (Ausrede) ist
fadenscheinig.

– *to wear*
fadenscheinig – flimsy

You're not going to **wear** me **down**.
Du wirst mich nicht mürbe machen!

to wear down –
mürbe machen

You've **worn** a hole in your jacket.
Du hast die Tasche in
deiner Jacke durchlöchert.

– *to wear out*
durchlöchern – to wear through

That's a **weight** off my mind.
Mir fällt ein Stein vom Herzen.

– *weight*
der Stein – stone

You're **welcome** to use it.
Du kannst es gerne benutzen.

– *welcome*
gerne – gladly

You did as **well** as you could.
Du hast es so gut gemacht, wie du es konntest.

well – gut

Well! **Well!**
Na, ja!

well – na, ja

You would do **well** to say nothing!
Es wäre besser, nichts zu sagen!

– *well*
besser – better

It's just as **well**.
Es ist ebensogut.

– *well*
ebensogut – just as well

You don't know when you're **well-off**!
Du weißt ja nicht, wann es dir
gutgeht!

– *well-off*
gutgehen – to go well

You **wet** (past tense) the bed.
Du hast ins Bett gemacht.

– *wet*
machen – to make

195

VW VW VW VW VW VW VW VW VW VW VW VW VW

Who **whacked** you over the head?   to whack – schl<u>a</u>gen
Wer hat dich auf den Kopf geschl<u>a</u>gen?

What will people say?   what – was
Was w<u>e</u>rden die L<u>eu</u>te wohl s<u>a</u>gen?

What about me?   what – was
Und was ist mit mir?

What next!   what – was
Was kommt jetzt!

What you see is **what** you get!   what – was
Was du siehst, das bek<u>o</u>mmst du!

Take **what** you want!   what – was
Nimm, was du willst!

So **what**?   *– what*
Na, und?   und – and

What a lot of water/ money!   *– what*
So viel W<u>a</u>sser/Geld!   so viel – so much

What about a game of soccer?   *– what*
Wie wär's mit <u>ei</u>nem F<u>u</u>ßballspiel?   wie – how

What good is that?   *– what*
W<u>e</u>lchem Zweck s<u>o</u>llte das d<u>ie</u>nen?   der Zweck – purpose

I'm going to give you **what for**!   *– what for*
Ich sag's dir war<u>u</u>m!   war<u>u</u>m – why

Do **whatever** you like!   whatever – was
Mach, was du willst!

VW VW VW VW VW VW VW VW VW VW VW VW VW

Whatever you say...
Was immer du sagst....

whatever – was

Say when!
Sag, wenn's soweit ist!

when – wenn

Where did I go wrong!
Wo bin ich verkehrt gegangen!

where – wo

Go **where** you like!
Geh, wohin du willst!

– *where*
wohin – where to

Whether you come or not, we shall leave.
Es ist egal, ob du kommst oder nicht, wir gehen fort.

whether – ob

While you're at it...
Während du dabei bist....

while – während

Don't go just on a **whim.**
Geh bloß nicht, weil du so gelaunt bist.

– *whim*
gelaunt – in the mood

Stop **whining!**
Hör auf zu jammern!

to whine – jammern

Give it a **whirl!**
Probier es mal aus!

– *whirl*
ausprobieren – to try out

Speak in a **whisper!**
Sprich im Flüsterton!

whisper – der Flüsterton

Who do you think you are?
Was glaubst du, wer du bist?

who – wer

Open your mouth **wide!**
Mach den Mund weit auf!

wide – weit

VW VW VW VW VW VW VW VW VW VW VW VW VW

You're not going to run **wild**
while we're gone.
Du wirst nicht außer Rand und Band sein, während wir weg sind.

wild – außer Rand und Band

I'm not **wild about** our going.
Ich bin nicht gerade begeistert davon, daß wir gehen.

wild about – begeistert von

Where there's a **will** there's a way.
Wo ein Wille ist, ist auch ein Weg.

will – der Wille

God **willing**.
So Gott will.

– *willing*
wollen – to want

You **win** hands down!
Du gewinnst eindeutig!

to win – gewinnen

Win some lose some.
Mal gewinnen, mal verlieren.

to win – gewinnen

You just can't **win**.
Man kann es nicht jedem
gerecht machen.

– *to win*
gerecht machen – to make fair

She **winds down** (lowers) the (car)
window.
Sie kurbelt das (Auto)Fenster herunter.

to wind down –
herunterkurbeln

We wind up (raise) the (car) window.
Wir kurbeln das (Auto)Fenster hinauf!

to wind up, raise –
hinaufkurbeln

Don't try to **wing it**!
Versuch es nicht, wenn du keine
Kenntnisse hast!

– *to wing it*
die Kenntnisse – knowledge

Wipe your nose!
Putz dir die Nase!

to wipe – putzen

198

VW VW VW VW VW VW VW VW VW VW VW VW VW

It wouldn't be **wise** to do it.   wise – klug
Es wäre nicht klug, es zu tun.

Wise up!   to become wise – vernünftig werden
Werde vernünftig!

Wish you were here.   to wish – wünschen
Ich wünschte, du wärest hier.

As you **wish**.   *– to wish*
Wie du willst.   wollen – to want

What more could you **wish**/ ask for?   to wish for – sich wünschen
Was könntest du dir noch wünschen?

I'm **with** you! (agree, support)   with – mit
Ich bin mit dir einverstanden!

I'm not **with** you. (Uncertain)   *– with*
Ich kann dir nicht folgen.   folgen – to follow

Keep your **wits** about you!   *– wits*
Halte deine Sinne beisammen!   der Sinn – sense

You seem a little **wobbly**.   wobbly – wackelig
Du scheinst, etwas wackelig auf den Beinen zu sein.

Don't cry **wolf**!   *– wolf*
Schlag keinen blinden Alarm!   der Alarm – alarm

I **wonder** about you sometimes.   to wonder – sich Sorgen machen
Ich mache mir manchmal Sorgen über dich.

No **wonder** you didn't get it done!   wonder – das Wunder
Kein Wunder, du hast es nicht geschafft!

VW VW VW VW VW VW VW VW VW VW VW VW VW

Don't say another **word**!   word – das Wort
Sag kein weiteres Wort!

Not a **word**!   word – das Wort
Kein Wort!

Tell me in your own **words**!   word – das Wort
Sag es mir in deinen eigenen Worten!

You took the **words** right out of my mouth! word – das Wort
Du hast mir das Wort aus dem Mund genommen!

Always keep your **word**.   word – das Wort
Man soll immer sein Wort halten.

You went back on your **word**!   word – das Wort
Du hast dein Wort nicht gehalten!

Don't put **words** in my mouth.   word – das Wort
Dreh mir nicht das Wort im Mund herum!

I'll take your **word** for it.   word – das Wort
Ich nehme dich beim Wort.

I'll put in a good **word** for you.   word – das Wort
Ich lege für dich ein gutes Wort ein.

Word for **word**!   word – das Wort
Wort für Wort!

A **word** of advice…   – *word*
Ein Ratschlag....   der Ratschlag – a piece of advice

A **word** of warning!   – *word*
Laß das dir zur Warnung dienen!   die Warnung – warning

200

VW VW VW VW VW VW VW VW VW VW VW VW VW

You **work** like anything for money!   to work – <u>a</u>rbeiten
Du <u>a</u>rbeitest wie verr<u>ü</u>ckt, wenn's ums Geld geht!

Get to **work**!   work – die <u>A</u>rbeit
Mach dich an die <u>A</u>rbeit!

I put a lot of **work** into that.   work – die <u>A</u>rbeit
Da h<u>a</u>be ich viel <u>A</u>rbeit hin<u>ei</u>ngesteckt.

Let's get down to **work**!   work – die <u>A</u>rbeit
M<u>a</u>chen wir uns an die <u>A</u>rbeit!

Is this all your own **work**?   work – die <u>A</u>rbeit
Ist das <u>a</u>lles d<u>ei</u>ne <u>ei</u>gene <u>A</u>rbeit?

It's all in a day's **work**.   work – die <u>A</u>rbeit
Es geh<u>ö</u>rt zur T<u>a</u>gesarbeit.

Many hands make light **work**.   – *work*
V<u>ie</u>le H<u>ä</u>nde m<u>a</u>chen ein schn<u>e</u>lles <u>E</u>nde.   das <u>E</u>nde – end

You have your **work** cut out for you.   – *work*
Du wirst schwer <u>a</u>rbeiten m<u>ü</u>ssen.   <u>a</u>rbeiten – to work

Work off your anger!   to work off – <u>a</u>breagieren
Reag<u>ie</u>r d<u>ei</u>nen Zorn ab!

We can **work** things **out**.   to work out – <u>au</u>sarbeiten
Wir k<u>ö</u>nnen <u>a</u>lles <u>au</u>sarbeiten.

It will all **work out**.   to work out, succeed – kl<u>a</u>ppen
Es wird schon <u>a</u>lles kl<u>a</u>ppen.

You're **working** your way **through**   – *to work through*
that book fast.   v<u>o</u>rwärtskommen – to move forwards
Du k<u>o</u>mmst mit dem Buch schnell v<u>o</u>rwärts.

201

VW VW VW VW VW VW VW VW VW VW VW VW VW

You've **worked up** an appetite!
Du hast dir Appetit gemacht!

– to work up
machen – to make

You're all **worked up** over it!
Du hast dich darüber sehr aufgeregt!

to be worked up –
sich aufregen

It's not the end of the **world**.
Davon geht die Welt nicht unter!

world – die Welt

I think the **world** of you!
Ich halte sehr viel von dir!

– world
halten – to hold, think

What is the **world** coming to!
Die Zukunft sieht nicht gerade
rosig aus!

– world
die Zukunft – future

The **worm** has turned!
Jetzt ist's umgekehrt!

– worm
umgekehrt – reversed, the opposite

What's **worrying** you?
Was bedrückt dich?

to worry – bedrücken

That's what **worries** me.
Gerade das beunruhigt mich.

to worry – sich beunruhigen

You needn't **worry**. I'll be fine.
Du brauchst dir keine Sorgen zu machen.
Es wird mir schon gut gehen.

to worry – sich Sorgen machen

You've got me **worried**.
Du machst mir Sorgen.

to worry – sich Sorgen machen

That's the least of my **worries**!
Das macht mir am wenigsten Sorgen!

to worry – sich Sorgen machen

VW VW VW VW VW VW VW VW VW VW VW VW VW

I was **worried** sick!   to worry – sich Sorgen machen
Ich habe mich vor Sorgen krank gemacht!

Not to worry!   worry – die Sorge
Keine Sorge!

Things are going from bad to **worse**.   worse – schlimmer
Es wird immer schlimmer.

It could have been **worse**.   worse – schlimmer
Es hat schlimmer sein können.

The **worst** is over.   worst – das Schlimmste
Das Schlimmste ist vorbei.

It's not **worth** it!   to be worth – sich lohnen
Es lohnt sich nicht!

This game is not **worth** buying.   to be worth – sich lohnen
Dieses Spiel lohnt sich nicht zu kaufen.

It's **worth** thinking about.   to be worth – sich lohnen
Es lohnt sich, daran zu denken.

Would you do it?   would – würden
Würdest du es tun?

I said, I **would** do it.   would – würden
Ich habe gesagt, ich würde es machen.

What **would** you have me do?   – would
Was erwartest du von mir?   erwarten – to expect

You're all **wrapped up** in   to be wrapped up – versunken
  your own activities.
Du bist in deine eigenen Tätigkeiten versunken.

VW VW VW VW VW VW VW VW VW VW VW VW VW

Don't get me wrong!   wrong – falsch
Versteh mich nicht falsch!

You were **wrong** not to tell me.   wrong – nicht richtig
Es war nicht richtig von dir, es mir nicht zu sagen.

You're going about it the **wrong** way.   wrong – verkehrt
Das machst du ganz verkehrt.

There's something **wrong**.   to be wrong – nicht stimmen
Etwas stimmt nicht.

Do you understand that you were wrong?   to be wrong –
Verstehst du, daß du Unrecht hattest?   Unrecht haben

It was bound to go **wrong**.   to go wrong – schiefgehen
Es mußte schiefgehen.

Y

Don't **yank** on it!   to yank – mit einem Ruck ziehen
Zieh nicht mit so einem Ruck daran!

Don't start playing **yet**.   *– yet*
Fang noch nicht mit dem Spielen an!   noch nicht – not yet

I can understand your friend,   you – du/dir/dich
but not **you**!
Deinen Freund kann ich verstehen, dich aber nicht.

My house is bigger, newer, and   your – dein/deine
better than **your** house.
Mein Haus ist größer, neuer und besser als dein Haus.

You told me **yourself**!
Du hast es mir selbst gesagt!

yourself – selbst

Did you do this by **yourself**?
Hast du es selbst gemacht?

yourself – selbst

You are not **yourself** today.
Du bist heute nicht auf der Höhe.

– yourself
auf der Höhe – at one's best

Pronunciation Guide

The following information is provided to give a basic understanding of correct German pronuciation. This guide should be considered only an approximation.

VOWELS

A: (short) as in *pond*. Example: Mann
(long) as in *father*. Example: Vati
(ä-short) as in *men*. Example: Äpfel
(ä-long) as in *pail*. Example: schärfen

E: (short) as in *bed*. Example: Essen
(long) as in *day*. Example: Weg
(unaccented) as in *ago*. Example: Bitte

I: (short) as in *it*. Example: Wind
(long) as in *feet*. Example: Hier

O: (short) as in *song*. Example: voll
(long) as in *foe*. Example: Boot
(ö-short) as *girl*. Example: Köchin
(ö-long) as in *early*. Example: hören

U: (short) as in *full*. Example: kurz
(long) as in *broom*. Example: ruhen
(ü-short) as in *pin*. Example: Küsschen
(ü-long) as in *feel*. Example: für

Y: same as ü. Example: Typ

COMBINATIONS

AU: as in *mouse.* Example: Maus
EI, AI: as in *sight.* Example: mein
EU, AU: as in *toy.* Example: neun

CONSONANTS

B: *b* as in *boy.* Example: beben
   p (at the end of a word) as in *map.* Example: gib

C: *k* as in *cold.* Example: Koch

CH: *kh* as in *huge.* Example: durch

CHS: *k* as in *socks.* Example: wachsen

D: *d* as in *dog.* Example: Bruder
   t (at the end of a word) as in *cat.* Example: Hund

G: *g* as in *good.* Example: tragen
   k as in *back.* Example: tag

H: *h* as in *hurt.* Example: Hand

IG: *ich* in North German pronunciation. Example: schmutzig

J: *y* as in *yes.* Example: ja

K: *k* as in *kick.* Example: Kuchen

L: *l* as in *light.* Example: lassen

M: *m* as in *mouse.* Example: Maus

N: *n* as in *not.* Example: nein

(cont.)

ŋ: *ng, nk* as in *sing, sink*. Example: singen, sinken

P: *p* as in *past*. Example: Panne

QU: *kv*. Example: Qualm (*kvalm*)

R: (rolled in the throat as in French or trilled at the tip of the tongue as in Spanish): Example: rot

S: *z* as in *is*. Example: lesen
   sh as in *should*. Example: spielen
   s as in *sing*. Example: das

ß is a double s sound. Example: Maß

SS: *s* as in *silly*. Example: Fuss

SCH: *sh* as in *show*. Example: Fleisch

T: *t* as in *tea*. Example: Zelt

V: *f* as in *father*: Example: Vati

W: *v* as in *visit*. Example: wir

Z: *ts* as in *sits*. Example: Zeit

* *

Also by Therese Slevin Pirz

Language Helper Series

Language Helper German
Language Helper Russian
Language Helper Angliiski
Language Helper Spanish
Language Helper Inglés

Kids Stuff Series

Kids Stuff German
Kids Stuff Russian
Kids Stuff Angliiski
Kids Stuff Spanish
Kids Stuff Inglés
Kids Stuff French
Kids Stuff Italian
Kids Stuff Chinese
Kids Stuff Yingyu (2008)

ABC's of SAT's: How One Student Scored 800
on the Verbal SAT